How We Pre-Empt the Onrushing Blowout

LaRouche PAC Issues Emergency Call To Pre-Empt Trans-Atlantic Economic Breakdown and Chaos

July 24—The LaRouche Political Action Committee issued an emergency call July 21, for a mobilization to pre-empt the chaos and devastation that will result across the Americas, Europe, and beyond, if measures are not taken immediately to initiate a Glass-Steagall re-organization of banking and credit, and proceed to a full economic recovery program as defined in Lyndon LaRouche's June 10, 2010 proposal, *Four New Laws to Save the U.S.A. Now! Not an Option: An Immediate Necessity.* This has now become a matter of life or death.

In a discussion with associates on July 20, Mr. La-Rouche said, "Wall Street *is* the problem. This is a key issue which must be pushed to the top, to be followed through, to prevent this danger to the economy as a whole."

As this issue goes to press, trigger points are lying in wait throughout the trans-Atlantic financial system, any one of which is capable of igniting and exploding trillions in toxic debt and unpayable claims—bringing down the entire financial system, and the physical economy with it. They include everything from the U.S. consumer debt bubble, to bundled auto loans, to corporate bad debt, and quadrillions of dollars of exotic financial derivative "products."

Perched at the top of this financial/monetarist nightmare is the Wall Street/City of London crowd, insisting that nothing needs to be done. They have lied—and continue to lie—that "we are past" the 2007-2008 crisis, that the "system is sound." Nothing could be further from the truth. In a recent discussion, Helga Zepp-LaRouche stressed that not only did the massive 2008 bail-out solve nothing—but it actually transitioned the system into a mode of accelerated looting of the population in the United States and Europe—looting the American and European people in a desperate attempt to try to maintain and continue this financial bubble. We are now reaching a new inflection point in that crisis.

The Reality

On any given day, look at the headline reports of the reality of the fragility of this system, and of the mass suffering it's causing!

In Italy at present, there is a criminal European Union "management" process of the so-called banking crisis under way, in which the EU is ordering a massive destruction of families' resources. Within the past few days, financial experts have warned that 16 out of 19 Italian banks that were tested, currently fail to meet the EU standards regarding non-performing loans. Instead of subjecting the Italian banks to Glass-Steagall reorganization (separating regular commercial banking from speculative practices), the EU has decreed a sell-off of the banks' non-performing loans (NPLs), in such a way as to drastically devalue the collateral behind them, which is often household and industrial real estate. Out of 88 billion euros of such collateral, an estimated 63 billion euros is expected to vaporize. This means the impoverishment of millions of families and businesses.

Take the example of Texas: On July 11, the *Houston Chronicle* reported that corporate defaults in Texas are higher today than they were during the 2008-2009 crisis. This includes some singular situations. One event described as "unheard of," was the collapse of a

Houston-based private equity fund called EnerVest, Limited, whose $2 billion valuation fell all the way down to zero. Prior to this, when a private equity fund went under, losses would typically max out at 25%. Here, we had a 100% loss. In its coverage, the *Wall Street Journal* interviewed experts who warned of the same danger at several other energy-focused funds.

Nationally, corporate default rates have continued to rise throughout 2016 and 2017. Auto loan delinquencies are now at a rate comparable to what mortgage delinquencies were in 2006, just prior to the mortgage bubble collapse. And on top of all of this debt lies a mountain of speculative "multiplier" contracts and "bundled securities."

It Is the People Who Suffer

In the United States, this month, the first group of retirees is getting slammed with drastic cuts in their pensions, under a measure signed by President Obama in 2014, called the "Multi-employer Pension Fund Reform Act" (MPFRA). In Ohio, retirees from Cleveland Iron Workers Local 17 are incurring pension cuts of up to 63% because, when their group pension fund faced bankruptcy—as many do because of economic decline—the Obama law demands cuts as the "solution," instead of using means such as the Pension Benefit Guaranty Corporation, set up in 1974 for just such contingencies. The ironworkers paid into their pension plan throughout their careers—some even took early retirement in exchange for the promise of a pension. Aging retirees are now plunging from the middle-class into poverty, with the threat of homelessness.

In the meantime, all across the United States there is a collapse of the physical infrastructure, from transportation, to water systems, to bridges. New York City is the international example, where chaos now threatens to erupt, as the subway, rail, and bridge systems experience almost daily breakdowns and crises.

It is the people who are suffering, whether it is through loss of their pensions, victimization by subway fires, or other infrastructure breakdowns, or seeing a loved one ensnared in the national drug-addiction epidemic, a product of our worsening cultural despair. This is not simply a banking crisis. It is a human crisis.

President Donald Trump was elected with an urgent mandate from the voters to stop the mass robbery, collapse, and rampant misery in the nation—and he has committed himself to Glass-Steagall and to major infrastructure investment. This can only happen if the Wall Street command-and-control over the economy and government is busted up. Timing is critical. September 30 is the end of the fiscal year for the Federal government and many corporate and other entities—a time when accounts are due, but, at this point, they are untenable. Even before that, in the first week of September, millions more passenger trips will be attempted in New York City as school opens. Will it be carnage?

Conceptual Breakthrough Required

The crucial change which must be made, lies in the way people think about economics. Almost no one in Congress, and very few individuals among the population, understand the issue of *Public Credit*, as it was defined by Alexander Hamilton, and as it was upgraded by Lyndon LaRouche. People look at what Abraham Lincoln built—such as the Transcontinental Railroad—or what Franklin Roosevelt built—such as the Tennessee Valley Authority—but people don't know how these things were done. It's just magic to most people.

For far, far too long, Americans have been brainwashed by the Wall Street-created phrase, "the independence of the markets," and—particularly since the repeal of Glass-Steagall—they have acquiesced in a surrender of the sovereign economic power of their own government—and to an orgy of useless, destructive financial speculation by the perverse controllers of Wall Street.

There are two lessons that must be learned: First, that the magnificent economic accomplishments of Hamilton, Lincoln, and FDR were all made possible by the sovereign imposition of a policy of *National Public Credit* for building up the real physical economy—such as transportation, energy, and water systems in great projects of economic development; and, Second, that there is no possibility whatsoever, that President Trump's stated desire to rebuild America's infrastructure and manufacturing can be realized without a return to just such an outlook and approach.

Emergency action is required, both in the United States and in Europe. Bold action! Such action, beginning with the reinstatement of Glass-Steagall, must be taken now, prior to an otherwise inevitable financial crash. Pre-emptive action, as defined by Lyndon LaRouche, is the order of the day. Our actions now are the deciding factor.

EIR Contents

www.larouchepub.com Volume 44, Number 30, July 28, 2017

Cover This Week

President Franklin Delano Roosevelt in 1941.

A New Banking Crisis by Year's End?
Savers and Pensioners Will Be Ripped Off!

by Helga Zepp-LaRouche, chairwoman of the German political party,
Civil Rights Movement Solidarity (BüSo)

WIESBADEN, July 22—There are growing signs that the 2008 banking crisis threatens to be repeated on an even grander scale—with the difference being that the "toolbox" of the central banks is now empty. That's because all of the so-called tools—such as quantitative easing (money-printing), and zero or negative interest rates—have been implemented for years without solving the underlying problem of the casino economy.

creative commons/Petar Milosevic

Bail-in "rescue": Banca Monte dei Paschi di Siena in Pisa.

The current policy benefiting the bankers and speculators—which continually widens the gap between rich and poor—represents the greatest threat to the general welfare, and thus to the stability of society itself. Only the immediate introduction of Glass-Steagall banking separation internationally, and a credit system that exclusively finances the real economy, can avert the danger of an uncontrolled collapse.

Although the government, the parties in the Bundestag, and mainstream media give the impression that the 2008 systemic crisis has done no lasting damage, and Fed chairman Janet Yellen even asserts that we will not experience such a crisis again "in our lifetime," the opposite is true. The trans-Atlantic world is sitting on a monetary powder keg, which can be set off by any one of a number of already burning fuses. Meanwhile the system continues to function according to the maxim, "profits are private, and losses are socialized"—that is, shifted to the so-called little people.

Two Ominous Examples

In the Rust Belt of the American Midwest, whose population has already been hit by the consequences of the globalization policy, pensions are being cut for millions of pensioners. Steelworkers, teamsters, office and factory workers, masons, and construction workers are threatened by cuts that would halve their old-age pensions for the rest of their lives. Responsibility for this lies with a law called the Multiemployer Pension Fund Reform Act (MPRA), signed by President Obama in 2014. The pension funds have been depleted, according to Joellen Leavelle, communications and outreach director of the Pension Rights Center, which she blames, among other things, on the 2008 crash which inflicted losses on many pension funds from which they have never recovered. Fewer next-generation workers, low interest rates, and the results of relocating production to cheap labor countries are other factors.

Another example is provided by the way the European Union (EU) and the Italian banks are fleecing their modest savers. It has been announced that 16 of the 19 Italian banks tested are not in compliance with European regulations with respect to their non-performing loans (NPLs). Under EU regulations, these banks are supposed to recapitalize by raising 32 billion Euros—either through the sale of the bad loans or through state aid. But state aid comes at the sole expense of the taxpayers, and not without "burden sharing," a kind of "bail-in light," by which shareholders and holders of contingent convertibles are expropriated. This procedure has just been used to rescue Monte dei Paschi di Siena (MPS) under the rubric of "preventive recapitalization."

It will be difficult to sell the bad loans on the open market: Since a fixed deadline has been imposed for meeting these demands, and market conditions are extremely bad, the NPLs might have to be sold at only 11 to 13% of their nominal value. The collateral for many of the loans was home or apartment mortgages, and prices for Italian homes and apartments have collapsed by around 50% since 2011, thanks to measures taken by the Mario Monti government. As a result, the market environment for selling NPLs is extremely bad. Moreover, the sale of a huge amount of real estate—it is estimated that real estate valued at 88 billion euros has been thrown on the market—will depress property values even further.

Because Italians normally invest the greatest part of their savings into their homes—much more so than in Germany, for example—the collapse in value is for them very serious indeed. The chief executive of Unicredit, Jean-Pierre Mustier, announced that his bank had completed the first phase of the selloff of its NPLs, which amount in total to 17 billion euros, at 13% of their nominal value, to international funds, which are also called vulture funds because of their business practices. Depositors not only lose their savings, but also their houses and apartments, while the vulture funds rake in the profit.

In the latest Italian bank resolutions, the EU Commission allowed state assistance—meaning tax money—in the amount of 5.4 billion euros, for Monte dei Paschi di Siena. In the case of two smaller banks, Veneto Banca and Banca Populare di Vicenza, the EU Commission has also allowed them to be saved according to Italian regulations. Austrian Finance Minister Hans Jörg Schelling sharply criticized this special treatment

Wikimedia Commons/Armin Kübelbeck
Wolfgang Schäuble, German Finance Minister: special treatment for troubled Italian banks.

for Italy, and stressed that the Austrian Hypo Alpe Adria is the only bank that has so far been resolved under European regulations. Looking at the long list of violations of the EU's rules, it is clear that the EU's insistence on being the only institution to set the rules is only a pretext. In reality, this argument is only put forward to curb China's influence. Interestingly, Finance Minister Wolfgang Schäuble sees no problem when EU rules are ignored in the case of Italy.

The Derivatives Threat

The Italian banking crisis is only one of the various landmines that could explode the whole system, because the total amount of bad loans in the European banking system is valued at one trillion euros. The much larger problem is the outstanding derivatives contracts, in which case the EU, wondrously, does not insist on its own regulations, but allows the banks to operate and balance their books according to their own models and using their own in-house algorithms.

Officially, the total volume of these derivatives comes to about $700 trillion, but in reality it is more than double that amount. If there were a sharp decline in one section of the market, it would risk setting off an international chain reaction. At the end of 2016, the

© European Union 2017
European Central Bank (ECB) President Mario Draghi: ECB interest rate still set at zero percent.

Office of Financial Research (OFR), a division of the U.S. Treasury Department, announced that the so-called "U.S. global systemically important banks" (G-SIBS)—the U.S. banks with global systemic influence—had more than $2 trillion in open positions in Europe. Approximately half of these positions are off-balance-sheet contracts. The OFR further emphasized that nine large banks in the United States and Europe are counterparties for approximately 60% of the $2 trillion in derivatives that American life insurance companies hold.

The real Achilles heel of the trans-Atlantic financial system is the derivatives bubble combined with corporate indebtedness. The corporate indebtedness of companies outside the financial sector has grown around 40% since 2008, as they used the abundant zero-interest-rate liquidities to buy up their own stocks, thereby driving up their nominal worth. The International Monetary Fund itself warned, in its recent semi-annual report, that even the slightest further increase in interest rates could result in a bankruptcy rate of more than 20% among U.S. corporations. That is the deeper reason why European Central Bank (ECB) President Mario Draghi has again set the ECB interest rate at zero percent.

The citizens would do well to realize how brutally pensions in the American Midwest are being halved and the Italian depositors are being expropriated. If a huge crash comes—as the threatening signs increasingly indicate—the life savings and the subsistence of the people will be ruthlessly sacrificed.

The Way Out

There is only one solution: The trans-Atlantic financial system must be totally reorganized in every country with a Glass-Steagall banking separation law, before a collapse occurs.

The EU's austerity policy has slashed the economy and the living standard of Greece by a third, and has dramatically increased the poverty rate; it is largely responsible for a similar development in Italy. According to reports of the Cologne Institute for Economic Research, poverty in Greece rose by about 40% from 2008 to 2015. The reports include not only income, but also material privation, underemployment, and cutbacks in health care. In Italy, poverty has nearly tripled over ten years. According to the Italian National Institute for Statistics (ISTAT), the number of Italians living in absolute poverty increased from barely 1.7 million people in 2006 to 4.7 million in 2016. That amounts to 7.9% of the population. In Germany, the Paritätische Wohl-

Xinhua/Chen Cheng

A May 12, 2017 photo of the Mazeras Bridge of the new Mombasa-Nairobi standard gauge railway in Kenya, constructed in cooperation with China.

fahrtsverband (Parity Welfare Association) reports that poverty stands at an historic high, at 15.7%, which means that 12.9 million people in Germany are poor.

Putting aside the obvious debate over how to define the concept of poverty, it is evident that the so-called winner country of globalization and the euro—that is, Germany—is in principle going the same way as Southern Europe, at least as concerns the underprivileged part of the population.

China's policy, which has not only freed 800 million Chinese from poverty but—through the New Silk Road policy—is doing the same for all countries cooperating with this project, stands in utter contrast. At a conference in Brussels on the theme, "The Future of Europe," Professor Michele Geraci of Nottingham University Business School briefly underscored China's role in the about-face on poverty in Africa. For centuries nothing had changed on that front, and in the 1990s the problem even got much worse. The western model, the "Bob Geldof Model," clearly failed miserably, he said. But today with Chinese investments, the poverty rate has dropped from 55% in 2000 to 40%

The people of Europe would undoubtedly be better off if China, not the EU, were defining the rules by which the economy functions. In any case, the BüSo's program—the enactment of the Glass-Steagall law and a credit system for the real economy, as well as German cooperation with the program of the New Silk Road—represents the only perspective for preventing the impending chaos.

Overflow San Francisco Event Points Toward Revolution in U.S. Economic Policy

by James Duree

July 22—A standing-room only crowd of 120-130 people met July 18 at San Francisco's beautiful War Memorial Building to discuss "China's Global Belt and Road Initiative—Will It Change the World?"

The War Memorial Building, across the street from City Hall, was the site of the signing of the United Nations Charter on June 26, 1945. The July 18 meeting marked a step forward in organizing the United States to join the international movement launched by China for the Grand Design of a World Land-Bridge.

The event was co-sponsored by the Schiller Institute and sections of the American Legion, including District 8, American Legion Cathay Post 384, and Post 448 (Veterans for Peace). The speakers were Lt. Col. Roger S. Dong (USAF-Ret.), Michael Steger of the Schiller Institute, and two diplomatic representatives: Sergei Petrov, the Consul General in San Francisco for the Russian Federation, and Sun Jia, Consul from the Consulate General of the People's Republic of China in San Francisco. Participating from the audience were representatives of other foreign consulates, news media, and prominent recent supporters of the Belt and Road Initiative (BRI). The diverse audience included many Chinese-Americans and U.S. veterans, along with fighters for the restoration of Glass-Steagall legislation and for Lyndon LaRouche's *Four Laws*.

The event was scheduled to begin with a reception at 6 p.m., followed by the actual proceedings starting at 7 p.m. But so many participants had already arrived by

EIRNS/James Duree

Participants in the July 17, 2017 conference in San Francisco, Calif.: "China's Global Belt and Road Initiative—Will It Change the World?"

around 6:15, that Lt. Col. Dong started playing a series of New Silk Road videos on the big screen at the front. They illustrated the development of the Chongqing industrial area in western China, a core part of the Belt and Road Initiative. The video presentation captured the imagination of the audience. As it ended, they erupted in spontaneous applause at a depiction of the future Land-Bridge connection of Eurasia to North America through the Bering Strait.

Speakers at the conference (at the table, left to right): Sergei Petrov, the Consul General in San Francisco for the Russian Federation; Sun Jia, Consul from the Consulate General of the People's Republic of China in San Francisco; and Lt. Col. Roger S. Dong (USAF-Ret.). Michael Steger is on the far left.

Lt. Col. Roger S. Dong

After the American Legion District 8 Commandant formally opened the event, a Schiller Institute vocal quartet led the audience in singing the National Anthem. Michael Steger then introduced Lt. Col. Roger S. Dong.

Dong, a Chinese-American veterans' leader with a long, worldwide career in Air Force Intelligence, gave a well-illustrated presentation on the Belt and Road Initiative. Dong discussed the issuance of public credit to build the New Silk Road, including the explosion in project financing by the Asian Infrastructure Investment Bank (AIIB) to $1 trillion. He stressed that the Belt and Road Initiative is already the "greatest economic and construction project in history."

Dong also emphasized that the "win-win" philosophy embodies the "New Paradigm" behind the Belt and Road. In conclusion, Dong displayed the Schiller Institute's World Land-Bridge map, from the 1997 *EIR* Special Report, and noted that the Schiller Institute "has been advocating this for twenty years," in reference to its intellectual authorship of the New Silk Road policy.

Only Development Can Eliminate Conflicts

The second presentation was by Consul Sun Jia, from the Consulate General of the People's Republic of China in San Francisco. His was of a distinctly different character, and began by discussing the philosophy of China behind the Belt and Road. Some of the most important captions from Sun's visuals follow:

1. "In the time of hardships, a man should seek self-development through efforts on his own, and in success, he should let others be benefitted." Mencius (372-289 BC). (This slide also had graphs of IMF GDP figures for key countries.)

2. "Why did China propose the Belt and Road Initiative?"

Answer: "A country should pursue prosperity and sustainable development while letting other countries live well."

3. "Best to be like water, which benefits all things and does not contend with them."

4. "How does the Belt and Road work?"

Answer: "Horizontal win-win cooperation of one's own accord, is the practice for implementing the Belt and Road Initiative."

5. "The Belt and Road Initiative, shining with the wisdom from the East, is a plan that China offers the world for seeking common prosperity and development."

His most important point was: "Only development can eliminate the root cause of conflicts, protect the basic rights of the people, and meet the people's yearning for a better life." He added: "The Belt and Road will benefit regions that have:

- 63% of global population,
- 29% of world's output, and
- $2.1 trillion of GDP."

He showed a terrorist running in front of a fire in some conflict, juxtaposed to the famous NASA photograph of the Earth from space at night, with the caption: "1.2 billion people have no access to electricity."

Putin on Belt and Road

The Consul General of the Russian Federation in San Francisco, Sergei Petrov, made it clear that Russian President Vladimir Putin has unreservedly embraced the Belt and Road Initiative, and intends to integrate the Belt and Road with the Eurasian Economic Union program of Russia and other post-Soviet nations. Dong reported afterwards that many in the audience—especially the Chinese-Americans—were surprised, even shocked, to learn of Russia's full endorsement of the Belt and Road.

In addition to the old Silk Road, the Consul General alluded to the history of the "Tea Route." Russian fur traders used to obtain sea-otter fur in Alaska, and ship it to China, where it was highly prized. They returned with Chinese tea to sell in Russia and elsewhere in Europe.

Petrov discussed his recent meeting with a trade representative from the Russian Federal Republic of Tatarstan, and the related project of a Moscow-to-Kazan high-speed railway, which is projected to continue to Chelyabinsk, Russia, and from there to China. This is an aspect of Russia's involvement in the Belt and Road Initiative. The Consul General emphasized that "China invited us" to join the BRI, and that Russia's involvement in the Belt and Road is a "long-term, principled commitment."

Petrov invited all the participants to attend the coming "Vostochny" ("Eastern") Economic Forum in Vladivostok this coming September, and the St. Petersburg International Economic Forum (SPIEF) in May 2018.

He concluded by quoting a recent remark of President Putin's: "Let us pave this road to development and prosperity, together."

BRI Requires Hamiltonian Credit

The final report was by Michael Steger, Director of the Schiller Institute in the San Francisco Bay Area.

Steger had recently delivered a two-hour presentation on the Belt and Road at the Graduate School of Business at the University of San Francisco. He began his July 18 report with the shocking contrast seen by Schiller Institute founder Helga Zepp-LaRouche, in her 1995 visit to China—compared with her earlier trip there in 1971, during the Cultural Revolution. He played an excerpt of Zepp-LaRouche's famous introduction to the LaRouche PAC *World Land-Bridge* video. Helga says, "We will see how easy it is to change the world for the better." Steger emphasized the role of Lyndon LaRouche in forecasting in 1988 the end of the Berlin Wall, and the role of Mr. and Mrs. LaRouche in formulating the "Productive Triangle" concept as the initial bridge between East and West. He recalled their opening of the dialogue with China in the early 1990s, to emphasize the need to end geopolitics.

Steger focused on two key areas: (1) the astounding power requirements which will be needed to create and run the New Silk Road, and (2) why only a competent, Hamiltonian credit policy, with 1-2% annual interest rates and multi-decade maturities, could possibly fund these great projects. The contrary "bankers' arithmetic" approach, with its 10-12% interest rates, would result in paying back nearly $1 trillion over forty years, on a $10 billion loan! (Assuming a loan under such terms could ever be paid.)

How Do We Get This Done Here?

The first question to the speakers, expressing a common concern of participants, was, "So, how do we get the Belt and Road Initiative implemented here in the United States?"

Subsequent questions ranged from security concerns, to India's reservations on the BRI, to the crisis in the European Union, and the importance of fusion energy. Apparent throughout the discussion, was the wholesome shock-effect this well-composed event had had on their minds. Optimism ran through the discussion, as people grappled with the reality of the potential of the present historic moment. In particular, the interchange between the three groups—the veterans, the Chinese-Americans, and the LaRouche supporters—brought an entirely new dynamic to this event, portending additional openings for bringing the United States into full participation in the Belt and Road.

The Change that America Requires Now

The following edited transcript is composed of excerpts from the Monday, July 17 LaRouche PAC webcast, which featured Policy Committee members Diane Sare and Kesha Rogers, with host Matt Ogden. The discussion addressed the urgent need for the United States to implement Lyndon LaRouche's Four Laws, *and to do so now, before the impending blow-out of the trans-Atlantic financial system. Helga Zepp-LaRouche, founder of the international Schiller Institute, had made the point that President Trump's decision to meet with President Putin, and his ongoing work with President Xi, have created a great potential for the progress of mankind, but that the United States' economic collapse remains the Achilles heel of his administration, and it is up to the LaRouche Movement to address it.*

Matthew Ogden: If we use Glass-Steagall to shut down Wall Street and to dismantle this power center which has been so concentrated in Wall Street and in the City of London, then we will restore political power back to the Constitutional American System, and by so doing, we will free up the Presidency to act on these necessary policies, just as Franklin Roosevelt did. I think we'll get into it more, but it's a very nefarious role that's being played right now by Treasury Secretary Steve Mnuchin, one that the American people should be *very angry* about, and should be something that should be strongly denounced, as Lyndon LaRouche did when Mnuchin was originally appointed.

But there is nowhere where the immediate necessity for this kind of national mobilization for an emergency recovery program is more apparent than it is right now in the heart of New York City. So, I'd like to ask Diane to say a little bit about the situation there right now, and help to fill out this picture a little bit.

Diane Sare: I made a point a few weeks ago, as we were going into the Sylvia Olden Lee tribute that the Schiller Institute Chorus was involved in, that I had become very acutely aware of the crisis in the transportation system, because of the number of people showing up late for rehearsals. Then a couple of my colleagues blew out three tires in a pothole while driving from Staten Island, and I realized—just to take a step back and actually think about this—forget the individual incidents—what does this kind of incident indicate?

It demonstrates that the transportation infrastructure is old and has not been maintained. The rail tunnels crossing under the Hudson River were built in 1907, so they're one hundred ten years old. Some tunnels on the

Crowded 168th Street New York subway station, after a fire on the track blocked train traffic.

EIRNS/Diane Sare

East Side were built at that time or later—one in 1924. Therefore, you have infrastructure that's close to a century old, or even more than a century old. You have switches in the subways that were built in the 1920s and 1930s. You have a road system which is not being repaired in the way it should be, because of budget cuts: When you repave a road, you're supposed to start from the bottom, not just pick a particular pothole and fill it. So what we are looking at is a breakdown.

Moreover, the infrastructure we're using was not built for the population density that we have today. The traffic flow at Penn Station is almost triple—even before the so-called Summer of Hell began, where three out of twenty-one tracks are now closed for repairs. It was built for a capacity of about 250,000 commuters a day. Today, it is being used by 650,000. And every corridor in and out of Manhattan is similarly overloaded. You have something like 1.6 million people coming into Manhattan every day to work. It's only slightly less than that in the Summer.

I raised the question, as to what are the implications of this, and when I spoke with Mr. LaRouche about it, he said, "You need a committee," and one of the first things he outlined is that you need a forecast, you need a perspective on what will happen if this is not done. . . . I made the sort of obvious hypothesis: If you are trying to move 20% of the population on one overloaded corridor, into another corridor that's already over capacity, you are creating the conditions for a cascading series of breakdowns. And frankly, I probably underestimated, or wasn't even considering, the aging and crumbling of the entire grid—not just for transportation, but electricity and water also.

My [[video]] [[]] the other day, was not just about the subways, but the fact that people were late to chorus on Thursday night because there was a fire underground at 71st and Broadway—which was not connected to the subway system directly. But because it was a very hot day, the ground was hot; people were using a lot more electricity and whatever they coated the electrical wires with actually *melted,* so you had a fire which blew out electrical power in that area.

There was no electricity there for 24 hours. And then they were telling people, "we're turning it back on, but don't use the elevator, don't use things that really use a lot of electricity." This is *New York City* in the United States! Not a country that's been under so-called Third World conditions. In fact, rail expert Hal Cooper had made the point at a Manhattan meeting a few weeks

earlier, that one must remember that Manhattan is the economic center of the United States in many ways. A disruption of New York City would not only be devastating to New Yorkers, but would have a major destructive impact on the U.S. economy as a whole.

Now, what happened *just today?* There was a fire at 145th Street in the subway, which affected the A, B, C, and D Lines. This was supposedly a trash fire. People were stuck in a subway car for one and a half hours, twelve people were injured—people having panic attacks in the cars. I can imagine that: People being stuck in a subway tunnel with smoke billowing past them, and God knows whether they had air conditioning.

When I was in the subway the other day, there was no air conditioning, the car was massively overpacked, and the temperatures—people's glasses were steaming up, and there wasn't room to stretch your arms or move or do anything. So it's easy to see the panic that would set in if a car like that gets stuck in a dark tunnel, and the power goes out.

If something is not done to address this, there will be loss of life. And we are facing this all over the country! This is completely unacceptable. When these things get to that point, you risk having major upheavals, major chaos, but the population could bear hardship—not insanity, but hardship—if they knew there were a plan to address this.

Now, Lyndon LaRouche for the last 50 years has been doing *nothing but* producing such programs: He had programs *in the 1970s* for what should be done for Manhattan. Obviously, 40 years later, various things would be different, now, but the point is, these programs exist. So how do you get the funding?

We have engineers, we have talented people who could solve this. In Manhattan now, I think we may have to take drastic measures, like saying maybe people really should not come into the city, people should figure out how to work elsewhere. Maybe business owners should be compensated for not coming into their shops—I don't know. But I'm sure there are people who have expertise in these areas who could figure it out—maybe a plan already exists.

But the question is, *what is the future?* And I appreciate very much, Matt, that you began with talking about the Apollo mission, because *our nation used to think big.* China is thinking big; Russia is thinking big. The nations that have joined the Belt and Road are thinking fifty, one hundred, two hundred years into the future. Americans, with a bit of inspiration, would similarly think that way, and I would say, as Mrs. LaRouche said, Trump has done a brilliant job thus far with Russia and with China: We are on a pathway hopefully to being able to put the threat of thermonuclear war behind us—I wouldn't say it's completely behind us yet, and especially with the potential blowout of the financial system, it's definitely not behind us!

But, we have to get a program now, in the United States, based on what Lyndon LaRouche said, shaped by the knowledge that human beings are not beasts, that we are creative, that our contribution to society is through creative discovery, and the economic model for best reflecting that is what Alexander Hamilton did here in Manhattan and as Secretary of the Treasury, based on his conception of our Constitution, what he wrote in the *Federalist Papers*. Today there are certain very concrete measures that have to be taken. The first step is Glass-Steagall. But my concern is that the American people actually begin to think about this from the top down, and not from the bottom up.

Relevance of the Space Program

Kesha Rogers: Some people may not realize it, but this Thursday [July 20] is the forty-eighth anniversary of the Apollo 11 Moon landing. This should really give us an inspiration to emulate the mission and the potential that is now being unleashed by the new policy direction that China is taking internationally, including the cooperation that's now under way between China with President Xi Jinping and the United States with President Trump. Despite the hysteria and diversions to pre-

Neil Armstrong/NASA

Buzz Aldrin on the Moon during the Apollo 11 flight.

NASA

Mission Operations Control Room on July 24, 1969, celebrating the successful conclusion of the Apollo 11 lunar landing mission.

NASA

Apollo 11 mission—the first U.S. lunar landing—being launched by this Saturn V rocket on July 16, 1969.

vent cooperation between Trump and President Putin, we're finding that they are determined to make sure that this collaboration between Russia and America also moves forward, and as was indicated before, this *is* the way that we're going to prevent nuclear war, by having these missions work together.

I want to emphasize the importance of Mrs. LaRouche's remarks to associates yesterday. It's very important that this organization, the LaRouche movement, is living up to its historical mission. I think that challenge also has to be put to the United States government and to the American people directly. Because we do have an historic mission, and that historic mission was beautifully captured in the optimism of President Kennedy's space program. That wasn't something that was just a project in and of itself, but it came about because John F. Kennedy was a visionary.

We're talking about a matter of life and death for the people of this nation and for mankind. The progress of mankind is going to depend returning the United States to an American System, which is exemplified in Lyndon LaRouche's *Four Laws*.

As LaRouche understands from the standpoint of economics—we've been emphasizing this in recent discussions—the center and basis of that return to the American System has to be the creative human mind. That will enable us to rebuild our industrial capabilities and our transportation sector, and to re-establish our space program. It's not just a matter—as Diane explained—of saying, "we have to put the tracks back together on existing railways." We have to have a policy driver for saving the lives of the American people, making sure that we build up

Xinhua/Xing Guangli

China's new bullet train "Fuxing," pulling out from Beijing South Railway Station, June 26, 2017. The new-generation train has a top speed of 400 kilometers an hour, and a consistent speed of 350 km an hour.

our industrial and transportation sectors, and increasing the energy-flux density of our economy. To increase energy-flux density we must have a fusion power crash program—as stated in LaRouche's Fourth Law—along with our space program. Railways and high-speed rail systems can be built within this policy framework. China has accelerated its rail building program since 2007, when it had 78,000 km of rails. I believe there are now more than 124,000 kilometers of rail just within China. We can do this. We can absolutely do this.

I want to make this point: As I reflect on Mr. LaRouche's initiatives over decades, I see that he always emphasized the spiritual imperative in a Moon-Mars colonization program, and in space exploration and colonization more broadly. And that is what we are fighting for in a physical economic shift. This gets to the question of humankind's capability for creative reasoning, which allows us to conquer, to explore, to solve any problems put in front of us. We're facing right now the product of bad political decisions, bad economic decisions—going with the system of monetarism over what Alexander Hamilton set as a true system.

LaRouche captures it very beautifully—and this is the spark of optimism that we should have in our economic program, and in our space program—when he says, "The divine spark of reason. This spark enables each of us to develop the power of creative reasoning; the quality of reasoning typified by the work of the best scientific discoverers. Such persons are potentially of great benefit to both contemporary society and future generations." He says, "One new useful idea discovered by such an individual mind is of benefit to all mankind."

So, this is what we need right now—the creation and promotion of new discoveries, new ideas; an increase of energy-flux density through a fusion economy platform. We can't go piecemeal in building up the economy. We have to have an approach from the Solar System down.

This is the challenge right now, as we've said to President Trump. As Mrs. LaRouche has made clear—and we understand—this challenge is absolutely imperative and critical in the fight against the British Empire to enable strategic collaboration among nations, which is absolutely necessary. The key thing right now is that we have to break with the monetary system now; we have to restore to the country its mission.

President Trump has announced a very optimistic vision for the space program and has now named Scott Pace to head the National Space Council. I don't have much to say about that right now. What I do want to say is that we're going to restore our commitment to our space program as a national mission. It has to be based on the idea of bringing fully into effect Lyndon LaRouche's *Four Laws*, with the restoration of the Glass-Steagall Act being the first step, and a national credit policy that will enable us to fully fund a space program going in the direction that it should be going.

People should be absolutely optimistic, but also have the fighting spirit that this is the future that we want to create.

Sare: We had a discussion here this morning that I think was really useful, because people do have to think about where we are, actually. We were discussing with some of our Baby Boomer-aged organizers the conditions of life when they were young, compared to the conditions of life when a young person is working today. One person said that when she first started working, minimum wage was $2.50 an hour, and she worked a 40-hour week, and the rent for a two-bedroom apartment with living room, dining room, etc., was $97 a month. So, basically, with one week's pay at minimum wage, she could afford to pay the rent for that apartment, which she shared with her husband and maybe one other person.

Today, the minimum wage maybe is $10, in some places it might be $15, but the rent for that same apartment would be about $2,000. So you're talking about an increase in the minimum wage which might be four- or five-fold, but the rent is actually 20 times more than it was before. I think you'll find similar conditions even,— I was thinking about when I was a kid when, on a hot summer day in the mid-1970s, you would go down to the corner to buy an ice cream cone that was 30 cents. Today that same ice cream cone is $5; so it's a spectacular increase. Every single member of the population is going through this.

A tiny handful, probably a tiny fraction of the upper one percent, have gotten fabulously rich—through criminal activities, laundering of drug money, or simply ripping people off and looting them like the CEOs of our major insurance companies, or through activities like those of George Soros—and probably couldn't care less about what has happened to the people.

Every single person that we're talking to is feeling—apart from the panic of potentially being stuck in the New York City subways—the panic that if the next paycheck doesn't come, they're going to be foreclosed on. Even if the next paycheck does come, they're choosing between their blood pressure medication and paying the utility bill. This is a very real situation.

That also has a totally demoralizing and devastating effect on Americans. It's been a standard that you're supposed to be able to support a family. Nowadays, really, you can't. So, does that mean you're a bad person, a criminal person, a foolish person, an incompetent person? Well, since there's no discussion of the actual magnitude of the economic collapse we are currently experiencing, many people have concluded, indeed, that they are hopeless. So they turn to alcohol, they turn to drugs; they get a painful injury and they're prescribed opioids which make them feel better and make the pain go away; then they find themselves addicted. There's an enormous amount of stress which people are under, which translates into very short tempers, so there is an increase in road rage. You see the whole society affected by this.

President Trump has expressed that he wants to rebuild America, but you have very problematic characters like Treasury Secretary Mnuchin, who is totally opposed to this it. That's the urgency behind our mobilization.

I've used this image before, but I think it's very important now: When Franklin Roosevelt gave his first inaugural address, Labor Secretary Frances Perkins vividly describes looking out over the Mall in Washington—everyone was in tears. Why? Because Herbert Hoover had had his "chicken in every pot" polemic; things were terrible. We were in a depression, but the leadership of the country had been denying the reality. So Roosevelt's first step was to say "No! We are in a severely difficult time, but this problem is not a natural disaster that we cannot solve. The cause of this catastrophe is the money-changers; it's an economic policy which I, your President of the United States, am going to address. It's not going to be easy; we're not going to solve it instantaneously; but we can solve this together now."

The people were greatly relieved and began to develop such trust in the President, that the nation was able to move forward in a largely unified fashion. There were fights; there were agent operations, as we know. There was an attempt to assassinate FDR before he was inaugurated. But the point is that leadership inspired people, elevated them, elevated their thinking. That is the kind of thinking we urgently need today.

Ogden: That's the kind of intellectual ferment among the population which the activity of the LaRouche movement is catalyzing, and it is our responsibility to provide that leadership. That is what is required to secure a full victory in the very near term.

The Other Wall That Fell In Europe in 1989

by Claudio Celani

July 20—In 1989, along with the Berlin Wall, another wall was torn down: the wall separating traditional banks from investment banks. But, whereas the former ended an era of oppression for many peoples, the latter started another era of oppression.

In 1933, for the first time in the United States, President Roosevelt introduced the separation between banks of deposit and credit, and banks involved in financial trading. By so doing, he successfully protected depositors' savings, and permitted an unprecedented expansion of productive credit, thereby fostering the economic recovery of the United States. The U.S. model, called the Glass-Steagall Act, named after the two senators who had drafted it, was quickly imitated in many nations around the world, and facilitated the reconstruction and economic boom of western Europe after the war.

Under the bank separation system, no major financial crisis broke out. Failures of individual banks occurred in many nations, without ever jeopardizing the savings and credit system itself.

The abolition of bank separation in Europe preceded the official repeal of the Glass-Steagall Act in 1999 in the United States.

On Dec. 15, 1989, a little more than one month after the fall of the Berlin Wall, the European Commission issued Directive CE 646/89, which established that from then on, credit institutions could do all sorts of activities, including trading the entire spectrum of high-risk derivatives.[1] That directive bound all member countries of

Joyous celebration of the fall of the Wall at the Brandenburg Gate in Berlin in 1989.

the European Union to abolish their national regulations differentiating between the different types of banks—of which some regulations resembled the Glass-Steagall Act that established two categories of banks, while others separated banks according to short-term versus long-term borrowing and lending, and others simply separated savings banks as a special category.

The introduction of CE 649/89 occurred in the framework of the tumultuous events that followed the fall of the Berlin Wall and the strategic decision to accelerate the so-called "integration" process in Europe. The process of ceding sovereignty to the supranational institutions of the European Community had gone on for decades. The plan for the transition to a complete surrender of sovereignty to a European Union, with a Monetary Union, had been discussed for some time—but it had been kept on the backburner by justified national interests of European nations. The events of November 1989 accelerated that process: French President François Mitterrand, in agreement with British Prime Minister Margaret

---

deposits and other repayable funds from the public. 2. Lending. 3. Financial leasing. 4. Money transmission services. 5. Issuing and administering means of payment (e.g. credit cards, travellers' checks and bankers' drafts). 6. Guarantees and commitments. 7. Trading for its own account or for the accounts of customers in: (a) money market instruments (checks, bills, CDs, etc.); (b) foreign exchange; (c) financial futures and options; (d) exchange and interest rate instruments; and (e) transferrable securities. 8. Participation in share issues and the provision of services related to such issues. 9. Advice to undertakings on capital structure, industrial strategy and related questions, and advice and services relating to mergers and the purchase of undertakings. 10. Money brokerage. 11. Portfolio management and advice. 12. Safekeeping and administration of securities. 13. Credit reference services.

---

1. CE 646/89 is very explicit on what kind of activities "credit institutions" are allowed to perform. The annex lists them all: 1. Acceptance of

Thatcher, seized the opportunity as a geopolitical means of depriving a unified Germany of its sovereignty, and at the same time avert any pro-agro-industrial and pro-labor reconstruction of the economies of the post-communist countries.

Mitterrand had already reversed France's traditional Gaullist policy, which had opposed excessive transfers of sovereignty to European institutions. He had forced his own party to adopt the so-called "Europe 1992" plan, which was aimed at creating a Single European Market to eliminate trade barriers between European Commission (EC) countries by 1992. The EC is the executive of the European Union. When the Delors Commission (Jacques Delors headed the European Commission for three terms, including the period through 1989) pushed for a Monetary Union, Mitterrand backed it.

Mitterrand, a typical representative of French Social-Imperialism, followed geopolitical designs aimed at ensuring a French sphere of influence in an area stretching from continental Europe to North Africa and the Middle East. In this geopolitical design, however, France would play the junior partner to Britain, which had built the City of London as the real center of global financial power. Thus, the euro was promoted and backed by London and Paris as a geopolitical tool for controlling Germany and enforcing neoliberal policies to the advantage of financial markets dominated by London.

Germany had to be persuaded, by whatever means, to accept the euro/neoliberal blueprint for Europe. Deutsche Bank chairman Alfred Herrhausen, the most influential figure in corporate Germany, had a different idea. He had publicly proposed an anti-free-market dirigist economic development approach for the economies of East Germany and Poland, emphasizing the productive sector. Herrhausen's policy was consistent with the more ambitious proposal of Lyndon LaRouche for a European Productive Triangle.[2] Herrhausen was

From left to right: French President François Mitterrand, UK Prime Minister Margaret Thatcher, and German Chancellor Helmut Kohl.

assassinated on Nov. 30, 1989, physically eliminating the threat of his vision.

Two days earlier, Chancellor Helmut Kohl had presented his Ten-Point Program for the reunification of Germany: Points one, two and three of his proposal involved economic aid to East Germany for reconstruction and cooperation.

The day after Herrhausen's assassination, Mitterrand telephoned Kohl, telling him that he expected him to approve Mitterand's proposal for an Inter-Governmental Conference (IGC) on the Monetary Union at the coming European Council meeting in Strasbourg, Dec. 8-9. Kohl accepted on condition that the IGC would take place after his re-election.

The final communiqué of that European Council meeting did indeed draw a road map for establishing the European Monetary Union, starting from the coming Inter-Governmental Conference.[3] The first action of the European Commission was to issue CE 646/89, with the intention of tearing down the wall separating commercial banks from investment banks, thereby opening up national banking sectors to takeover by London-centered financial speculation. CE 646/89 was eventually incorporated into numerous other directives, and ultimately into the European Treaties in 2007.

The elimination of banking separation meant that only one type of banking model was admitted, the universal bank, under whose roof, both traditional deposit and lending activity takes place, as well as high-risk speculative activity. Investment banks that issue asset-backed securities could now rely on the protection offered by the commercial side of the bank, and on the entire savings of bank depositors as potential collateral for the expansion of the financial bubble. Suddenly, local savings banks would have to participate in derivatives trading on the global financial market. Banks started to merge and expand their balance sheets, grow-

---

2. See http://www.larouchepub.com/eiw/public/1990/eirv17n31-19900803/

eirv17n31-19900803_031-the_economic_geography_of_europe.pdf

3. See http://www.europarl.europa.eu/summits/strasbourg/st_en.pdf

ing larger and larger. Inevitably, the bubble burst in 2008, threatening the collapse of the entire system.

At that point, monetary authorities and governments used the blackmail of deposits being at risk, to implement the biggest bailout in history. Remember, that in the midst of that financial panic, German Chancellor Merkel and her Finance Minister, Peer Steinbrück, went on prime-time television to declare to the nation that "all savings and deposits are 100% guaranteed." But instead of doing the most reasonable thing, i.e. reintroducing banking separation and guaranteeing *only* deposits and savings, the German and most other EU governments also guaranteed that speculators would be bailed out.

Deutsche Bank Chairman Alfred Herrhausen.

It has been calculated that direct government bailouts of banks in the EU cost 800 billion euros. Germany alone paid 238 billion to bail out its banks; Spain 52 billion, Ireland 42 billion, Greece 40 billion, Netherlands 36 billion, Austria 28 billion, Portugal 19 billion and Belgium 19 billion. This massive bailout, financed with newly-issued government debt, only postponed the problem, and created another. Suddenly, the sovereign debt market in Europe was flooded with a giant supply, met by a relatively small demand. This forced countries including Italy, Greece, Portugal, and Spain, to offer higher yields to compete with German bonds. A European debt crisis developed which threatened to destroy the euro system itself. The first stage of the crisis was dealt with through so-called "bailout packages," carrying murderous austerity conditions. Greece's national economy was destroyed under this therapy.

In the longer term, to save the euro, the European Central Bank (ECB) started an unprecedented monetary expansion, buying sovereign bonds from the banks, and issuing special lines of zero-interest loans. Eventually, the ECB started buying corporate bonds and derivatives as well. Thus, its balance sheet was blown up to uncontrolled dimensions. At the end of 2016, the ECB balance sheet amounted to 3,661,439 million euros (3.6 trillion). The Eurosystem is *de facto* bankrupt.

All this would not have happened, if CE 646/89 had never been introduced.

And yet, all the measures taken since 2008—from government bailouts to central bank monetary expan-

sion—have failed to solve the problem. The overall debt has increased, while the real economy has stopped growing because of the austerity policy being implemented in the EU. The next explosion of the system is around the corner, even though monetary authorities have created the illusion that the system is "safer" through fake reforms such as stress tests and higher capital buffers.

In a further ceding of national sovereignty, banking supervision has been transferred from national central banks to the European Banking Authority (EBA), which is under the ECB. The EBA has conducted stress tests to simulate the effects of a crises on major EU banks. Banks that failed the test were ordered to increase their capital ratios.

However, the EBA has failed in assessing the real risk of megabanks' balance sheets, by allowing the banks to use their own internal models to assess the value of their financial assets. The most outrageous example is that of the so-called "Level 3" assets—toxic derivatives that have no market, and whose value is equal to zero. Yet the EBA has permitted the banks to declare an arbitrary value for those derivatives, turning losses into assets!

In April, the Italian Banking Association published figures for Level 3 assets in the EU, which show that the *highest ratio of Level 3 assets to capital* belongs to German banks, with 35.5%. Next come British banks, with 25.4%, and French banks with 20.5%. Italian banks, which are being vilified by the EU because of their losses on commercial loans, have "only" 15%.

In the case of Deutsche Bank, Level 3 assets amounted to 54.8% of tangible net worth!

While closing its eyes to toxic assets, the EBA is tightening the screws on commercial banks which are increasingly burdened by losses on their commercial loans because of the economic crisis. This has become acute in Italy; the Italian economy has suffered a severe recession due to the draconian budget cuts and tax increases imposed by the EU. It is calculated that Italian banks have about 400 billion euros in non-performing loans (NPLs).

The absurdity is that under EU law, it is impossible to recover an NPL. In former times, if a customer defaulted on a loan, the bank would try to negotiate measures with the customer to alleviate his economic condition, allowing him to pay back the loan in the near future. EU law prevents this, obliging banks to write off the asset and end any financial assistance to the customer—thus ensuring that the loan will never be repaid.

It is not difficult to see where all this leads: to the elimination of commercial banks as such!

The EU is not hiding the fact that this is its goal. Banks loaded with NPLs are told that they must change their "industrial model."

Whatever commercial banks survive this triage, will be finished by the next "reform": the Capital Market Union (CMU). Announced in 2016, the CMU is intended to replace bank loans with capital markets. In other words, firms will be told that if they need money to finance investments or trade deals, they must issue bonds on the market. In order to do so, they must turn to an investment bank, which will place those bonds. This ensures that smaller enterprises will be cut off from credit. In fact, only larger companies can afford both the minimal size of a bond issuance (5 million euros), and the fees charged by investment banks.

Reintroducing Glass-Steagall

In recent years, the call for reintroducing a bank-separation system has grown in Europe, especially among euro-critical and anti-establishment political forces. The campaign for Glass-Steagall has been especially strong in Italy, where many remember the 1936 Banking Act that had worked so well until it was formally abolished in 1995 by the Amato-Draghi reforms.

The cancellation of bank separation was the main cause for the crisis of Monte dei Paschi di Siena (MPS) bank, the third largest Italian bank and the oldest active bank in the world. Originally a commercial bank, MPS expanded into investment banking and into acquisitions, culminating in the leveraged purchase of Banca Antonveneta in 2008. In order to cover the losses from that purchase on its balance sheet, MPS then bought derivative contracts with Deutsche Bank and Nomura, which increased the losses. Eventually, the government had to

Italian Senator Oskar Peterlini

www.svpartei.org/de

© European Community/Christian Lambiotte

Former Italian Finance Minister Giulio Tremonti

EIRNS/Julienne Lemaître

Italian Member of European Parliament Marco Zanni

step in and *de facto* nationalize the bank in June 2017.

The banking crisis and the first implementation of the bail-in procedures have produced popular outrage and support for the reintroduction of banking separation. The first draft bill was filed by Sen. Oskar Peterlini in the Italian Senate in 2012. That bill was drafted together with *Movisol.org*, the LaRouche organization in Italy. In the following years, parliamentarians from almost all parties filed similar draft bills, both in the Chamber of Deputies and the Senate. Among them were prominent figures such as former Treasury Minister Giulio Tremonti. Finally, on March 16, 2017, the Finance Committee of the Chamber of Deputies began discussion of the eleven draft bills which had been filed, and decided to have hearings on the matter. That discussion has not yet been resumed, however.

In the European Parliament, the Italians Marco Zanni (Independent Party) and Marco Valli (M5S Party) began a fight for Glass-Steagall in the Economic and Monetary Committee. That fight was not successful, but it managed to prevent the two larger factions, the liberals and the social democrats, from uniting on an anti-Glass-Steagall platform.

But it is clear that a healthy banking system and issuance of credit to the economy can be re-established only under national law, repudiating and cancelling EU regulations. Step by step, the EU has built a system of financial feudalism which is destroying the real economy and impoverishing the population. It is necessary to reverse this process before the system collapses chaotically with devastating effects. European nations now have the unique historic opportunity to join the "One Belt, One Road" policy of economic growth initiated by China. In order to do that, they must re-establish national systems of credit.

How Adam Smith Fooled You Suckers Most of the Time

by Lyndon H. LaRouche, Jr.

In August 1956, I forecast that, somewhere near late February and early March of 1957, the U.S. economy would experience a deep, sudden recession. I traced the timing of that recession as to be centered in the practice of retail, new-car and used-car automobile marketing, which was being conducted under the credit policies of Arthur Burns, then Chairman of President Eisenhower's Council of Economic Advisors. It happened exactly when and why I had forecast this would occur. In the course of 1956, the 36th payment on the loan of a new automobile was a lalapalooza! The results soon showed.

Since then, I have employed what I had learned from that successful forecast for each and all of my long-term and related forecasts since that time. What I had forecast, in each case, had been a warning of a crucial "turning point," a choice of a branch in the road, as if between fame and folly, in exactly the same way I forecast the recent, and still continuing, general breakdown-crisis of which I had warned, on July 25, 2007, as I was then about to launch the design for my proposed Homeowners and Bank Protection Act of 2007.

As for my method for my forecasting, at that time, and since, it has always been based, since the early 1950s, on the powerful impact of Bernhard Riemann's habilitation dissertation on me, as if it had been, and actually was rooted in my adolescent and later exposure to the anti-reductionist method of Gottfried Leibniz.

I have never been in error in any forecast of crisis for the U.S. economy since the first, which I had uttered in August 1956. In the following report, (as the popular saying goes) "I reveal" the precise reasons why I have never failed in any forecast of that type which I have made since 1956, and through the present successful continuation of the current forecast, delivered on July 25, 2007.

Foreword:

The art of successful forecasting can only be acquired by way of that branch of physical science which may be described most conveniently as to be discovered through a detour into "hind-casting." The best choice of example of this approach, is to be recognized in the published accomplishments of Johannes Kepler, especially his uniquely successful discovery of the principle of universal gravitation, that as the relevant steps toward that success are detailed, still today, in his **The Harmonies of the Worlds,** and as the starting-point for beginning that stage of accomplishments is typified by his earlier **The New Astronomy**. Among the most famous of the discoveries which echo the root of Kepler's own such discoveries, was Carl F. Gauss's famous, uniquely original, pioneering discovery of the orbit of Ceres. A compact form of relevant tensor analysis of Gauss's discovery was provided by a member of my so-called "basement team," and has been available from that site (http://archive.larouchepac.com/tensors).

Notably, Kepler had defined the principled composition of the determination of the array of solar orbits, by the ironical juxtaposition of respectively visual and harmonic determination of the orbital array, thus employing the contradiction between those two contrasted kinds of sense-perception, to define a universal principle which was not defined by either of those two kinds of sense-perception.

Notably, all validated notions of universal physical principles are obtained by a method comparable to that employed by Kepler for this case. True universal physical principles, are not derived from the presumed authority of the experience of sense-perception as such, but are proven through study of the contradictions among the merely apparent principles of sense-perception. All lawful processes in the universe exhibit such effects; but, to the best of our present knowledge, only the creative powers specific to the individual human mind, are capable of recognizing such a principle as such as a universal principle, that in a willfully knowledgeable way. This distinction is to be associated with Academician V.I. Vernadsky's definition of the principle of the noösphere. Kepler follower Leibniz's original discovery of the principle of least action, has congruent conceptual implications, as does Bernhard Riemann's 1854 habilitation dissertation[1].

The human mind is not a product of sense-perception; rather, sense-perception is a tool employed by the human willful mind, a mind which encompasses human sense-perception, but is not encompassed by the latter. My own knowledge of the relevant matters addressed in this present report, was provided, most notably, by a view of Riemann's habilitation dissertation, which I knew as rooted in the same influence of Leibniz which I had encountered in my own studies.

The crucial relevance of my preceding remarks, here, for the subject of competent forms of economic forecasting, lies in an appreciation of the principles of a science of physical, rather than a monetarists' economy, an appreciation which was rooted most immediately for me, in my encounter with Bernhard Riemann's habilitation dissertation.

The failure which I have encountered among putative forecasters known to me as my opponents in economics, is to be located, chiefly, in the special relevance of the influence of the devotees of Aristotle, or of the "liberalism" of Paolo Sarpi, and of the pack of their followers.

Modern European styles in what have been, fairly consistently, failed forecasting methods, are expressed as the effects which are to be traced chiefly, today, in the influence of the form of so-called behaviorism specific to those followers of Sarpi and his lackeys, Galileo Galilei, Francis Bacon, and Thomas Hobbes whose influence is reflected in the Anglo-Dutch Liberalism of such as John Locke, Adam Smith, and Jeremy Bentham. I shall explain this, here, as follows.

Carl F. Gauss's uniquely original discovery of the orbit of the asteroid Ceres, echoes the method of Johannes Kepler's similarly original disovery of universal gravitation, made possible by the ironic juxtaposition of two kinds of sense-perception, vision and hearing (harmonics), neither of which, alone, were capable of making such a discovery.

---

1. *On the Hypotheses Which Lie at the Foundation of Geometry.*

I. Adam Smith's Brutish Principle

"To man is allotted a much humbler department .... Nature has directed us to the greater part of these by original and immediate instincts. Hunger, thirst,the passion which unites the two sexes, the love of pleasure,and the dread of pain, prompt us to apply those means for their own sakes, and without any consideration of their tendency to those beneficent ends which the great Director of nature intended to produce by them."

—Adam Smith
Theory of Moral Sentiments, 1759.

Adam Smith, when viewed in reference to his own close relationship to Lord Shelburne (William Petty) and to Shelburne's chief British Foreign Office lackey, Jeremy Bentham, points out the most relevant sampling in Smith's own 1759 book, rather than his later, 1776, notable expressions of plagiarism copied from the unfinished draft of A.R.J. Turgot's 1769 essay "Reflections on the Formation and Distribution of Wealth." That is to emphasize that the ***Moral Sentiments*** is the most relevant of Smith's writings for insight into the argument which later drew the British East India Company's chief executive, Lord Shelburne to his 1763 co-opting of Smith's assignment to spy against French and the American targets during that 1763-1776 interval. The excerpted passage, noted above, is an essential reference for my present report, that on account of the most direct and simple evidence of the causes for the failures of our contemporary forecasters generally.

Even a fair amount of reflection on the dogmas usually employed, canonically, for designing forecasts by economists today, reveals that they are plainly products of the equivalent of what Smith identifies, in the cited passage from his 1759 book, as his advocacy of a perfectly irrational pleasure-pain principle. Notably, Smith himself demands that man accept his insistence that there is no rational basis in reason for this presumed principle, beyond behavior typified by the equivalent of irrational prevalence of the irrationally presumed propensity to buy, sell, and consume. For Smith, there is, in short, no rational form of allowance among the liberal

The British East India Company's Adam Smith's (inset) insistence that man is a mere creature of his appetites, and his instinct to seek pleasure and avoid pain, is the basis for today's cultish belief among both economists and the general population in money and the "magic of the marketplace," i.e., Smith's "invisible hand." This engraving by William Hogarth, "Beer Street" (1751) satirizes the animal-like existence to which the English subjects of British Empire were reduced.

behaviorists for the role of the economic-productive process itself. Almost everything in economic life and related matters is referred by him to the utterly irrational "magic of the market-place." Little wonder, that not only does public opinion often fit the name of something akin to the "pubic opinion" of such as the late Walter Lippmann, but even legislative bodies tend, not infrequently, toward something of that sort of approach to law-making.

My own approach to forecasting, therefore, takes the form of man's willful actions on the productive processes of society, rather than the currently popular view of forecasting which presumes, under the silly, but virtually axiomatic presumptions of the behaviorists, that it is the unforeseeable motivations of the processes of production themselves, which generate the conditions

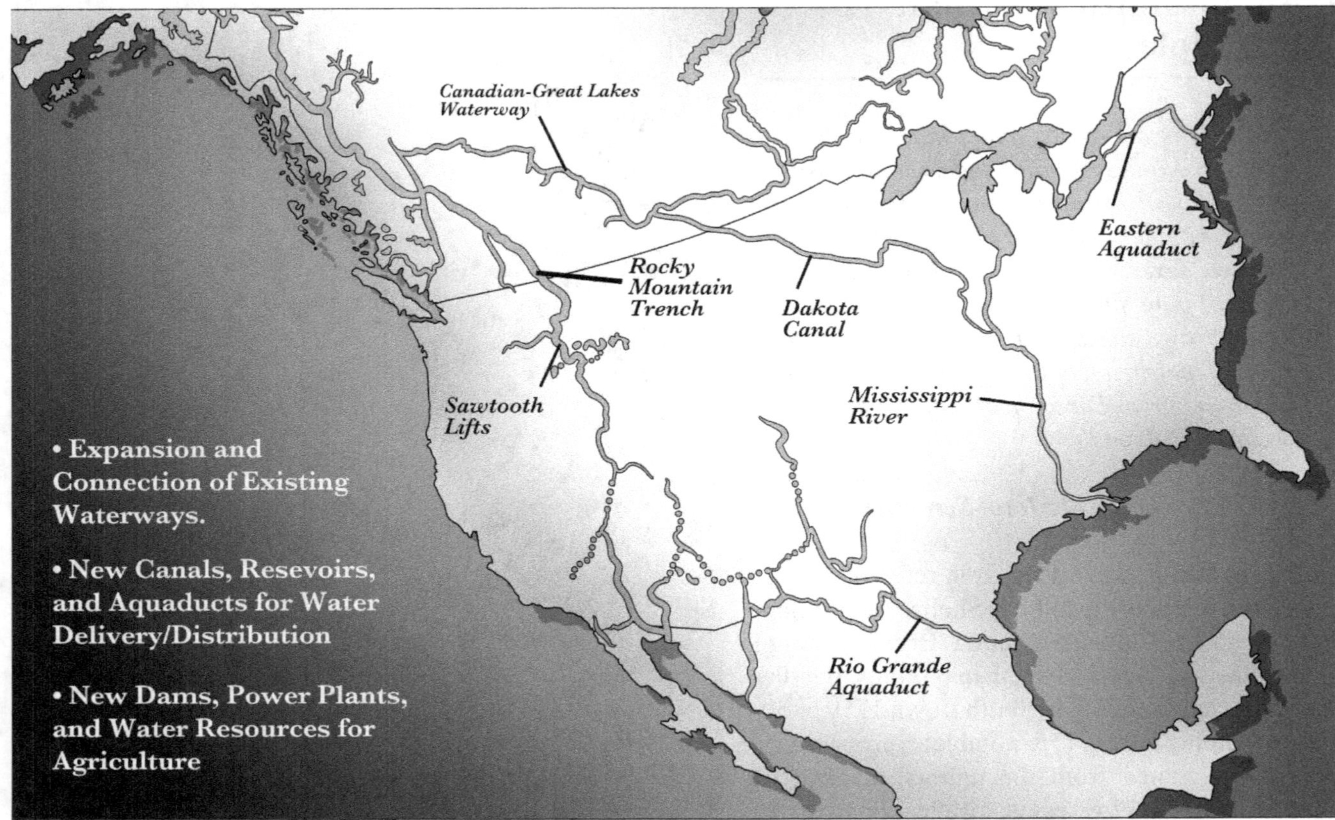

NAWAPA (the North American Water and Power Alliance), as LaRouche has conceived it, will link up with related great projects across the Americas, Eurasia, and Africa, leading to "a mighty, upward transformation of not only the present surface of our planet, but the foundations for mankind's development of relevant improvements in nearby Solar space."

to which, in turn, the irrational processes of public opinion react. For me, as a matter of contrast, the root of economic crises in societies, is to be found in a willful mankind's failure to understand the requirement for a willfully noëtic quality of lawful ordering within a successful development of the productive processes.

This noëtic characteristic of human creative behavior, is specific to the human will, but the same kind of principle is expressed, unconsciously, but efficiently, in such forms as the development of the Solar system, and the evolution of the lithosphere and biosphere of our planet Earth, as in the relatively exceptional case of the noëtic aspect of the conscious will of the human personality. Speaking plainly, the "Second Law of Thermodynamics" was always a hoax.

What I have just written here, thus far, brings us to the brink of what should be, for most readers, a rather startling paradox.

The Creative Role of Infrastructure

I have repeatedly emphasized, but, now more emphatically, the role of The North American Water and Power Alliance (NAWAPA[2]) as a key to any successful recovery program under immediately present conditions in the world at large, that the progress of actually net improvements in the human condition, has depended on a succession of "layers" of successively higher orders of "platforms" of basic economic infrastructure. That set of qualitative general improvements in the potential of the human condition, is typified by the order of trans-oceanic maritime cultures based on the "star map;" the development of riparian systems of interlinked rivers and canals, as in the work of Charlemagne for his reign's section of Europe; the development of not only railway systems, but the transconti-

---

2. The following report was subsequently published by LaRouche PAC.

nental railways systems which served as the perceived threat which was met by the British Empire's organization of World War I, World War II, and the nuclear-heated "Cold War;" and, now, British drives for its imperial system of "pro-genocidal globalization" such as the intention of the World Wildlife Fund to reduce a world population of now approaching seven billions people, to not more than two.

Presently, the model of President Franklin Roosevelt's TVA, is echoing still as the NAWAPA and related great projects for the Eurasian and African continents which represent a mighty, upward transformation of not only the present surface of our planet, but also the foundations for mankind's development of relevant improvements in nearby Solar space.

That succession of upward leaps in the global platforms of Earth's development, on which advances in the human condition depend, defines the kinds of technologies on which advance in the human condition depends, and which those advances demand.

It is these kinds of "platforms" on which both the possibility and the fruits of such leaps in human progress depend.

The success of the TVA under President Franklin Roosevelt's terms in office typifies the way of policy-making thinking which now represents the characteristic features of the great leap upward in progress needed for this planet as a whole today.

These "platforms" of successive phases of progress of the human condition, are the proper foundation for the crafting of the economic policies of nations now. That is to emphasize, that the productivity of a national economy, especially an economy composed of a number of national regions on the same continent, depends primarily on the potentialities defined by these platforms. The feasibility of progress in production and living standards themselves depends upon the role of the development of the "platforms." Even the possibility of the success of attempts at particular advances in productivity and standard of living of populations, depends on the progressive ordering of these platforms, primarily, and of technologies of production, secondarily.

These platforms, and their internal development, depend upon qualitative advances in technologies, in which qualitative increases in levels of applicable "energy-flux density" are primary increments of change.

That set of relationships within the process of attempted progress is essentially inseparable from the development of the platforms on which the general existence of a level of civilization depends.

The contrary consideration is expressed as the process of attrition which is inherent in any lack of development of an increased energy-flux density in the modalities of both the "platform" itself, and also the employed technologies.

These considerations define the "market," that in terms of the needed upward leaps in the platforms, and in the relative anti-entropy of the productive processes deployed.

In general, among rational and reasonably well-informed leaders in economies, the inevitability of necessary progress in forms typified by increase of energy-flux density, as toward nuclear-fission and thermonuclear-fusion power and beyond, employed for both infrastructure and production of consumable goods and of essential services, expresses the determinants of economic progress, determinants which, in turn, require correlated rises in the power expressed by the platforms themselves.

II. What Is Human Nature, Really?

In recent years, I have placed increasing importance on the role of distinguishing the "inner" quality of the individual human identity, from the commonplace banality of equating the mind of the human personality to attributes of sense-certainties. To this purpose, I have emphasized the several qualities of that expression of evidence which demonstrates that the human personality and the aspect of the human experience represented by sense-perception, can not be ontologically coincidental.

The case of Albert Einstein's appreciation of Johannes Kepler's uniquely original discovery of the general principle of gravitation, has the character of an essential empirical demonstration of my point here.

Notably, however, both the doctrines of Aristotle and Paolo Sarpi express the evil principle of the Apollo-Dionysian Delphi cult, which, in the symbolism of Aeschylus, defines mortal man and woman, as below the gods of Olympus, and defines the Mosaic and Christian God as rendered permanently impotent according to the thesis that "God is dead" once the original act of Creation had been created. Hence, Friedrich Nietzsche's "God is dead."

To present the relevant case which such cultural-

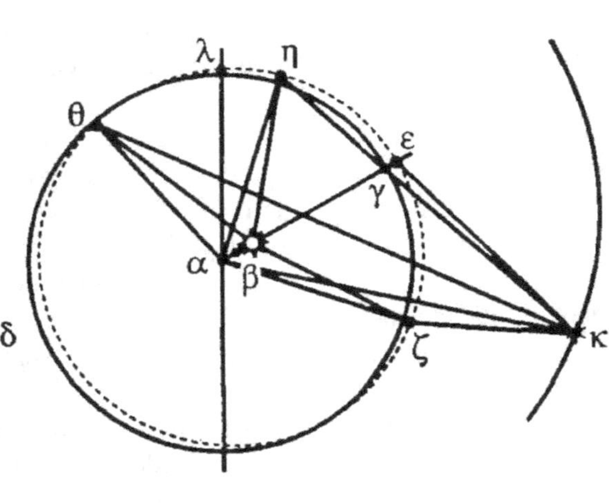

Ferdinand Schmutzer

In this diagram from his The New Astronomy (1609), Kepler used one repeated point in the Mars orbit, seen at different times from Earth, to reveal the motion of the Earth itself. Einstein recognized this as the work of a genius.

ideological facts imply, it is warranted to focus our illustration of the point upon the case of the European maritime cultures and their offshoots.

For this case, the history has been of recurring collapses of cultures since the case of reference represented by the decline and collapse of Sumer. In all of the better-known cases studied, the process of decline has been inherently a product of an oligarchical culture with characteristics congruent with the pattern of Aeschylus' ***Prometheus***.

Mankind is the only living species whose existence is as something tantamount to a "culture," which deliberately uses fire as an instrument of the capacity to survive and progress. In relevant cases of either myth or history, the acquisition of the power of the use of fire becomes a perceived threat to the political-social power by an oligarchy of "gods" over a population of virtual slaves and the like. The modern cases of Britain's Prince Philip and Prince Bernhard of the Netherlands in forming the International Institute for Applied Systems Analysis (IIASA)-related World Wildlife Fund and Club of Rome, are typical. So was the policy of the Hitler movement in its time, the policy of the W. Averell Harriman circles inside the U.S.A. in their time, and the anti-nuclear movement today.

While the oligarchical circles, the would-be "ruling gods of Olympus" reigning over the lower classes, do seek increased power, they fear the rise to power of the people more than they wish for the increased means of power of society to continue to exist. Such has been the policy of the inner circles of the Barack Obama Presidency, including such desperadoes as the Larry Summers of "Creative Destruction" notoriety. Such have been the policies of the British government under Prime Minister Tony Blair, and the similar programs of intended mass-murder among the citizens by the Obama Presidency thus far.

The case of the British empire's continuing tyranny over the continent of Africa, is a clear example of the same pro-oligarchical evil of those who join an Olympian Zeus as a self-appointed class of "gods."

That much said on background for the point being considered now, the essential practical point to be emphasized here and now, is that the justified expectation of an increase in the general welfare of particular nations, or mankind in general, demands a general rise in the effective energy-flux density expressed as the characteristic of a platform on which production and consumption, per capita and per square kilometer, depends. Regard this as a needed restatement of what has been named in past times as "the principle of limitless progress."

Otherwise, any effort to put a cap on the necessary rise of energy-flux density, and upon the related rise to successively higher qualities of historical platforms, means an inevitable collapse of any civilization into a long wave of entropic decline. It is the measures, to be taken, or to be avoided, for the sake of progress in the quality of cultural-economic platforms, as typified by the indispensable installation of Glass-Steagall and NAWAPA now, which define the indispensable current policy of any nation to be considered as actually a part of civilization.

THE GENERATION OF 'POET-MATHEMATICIANS'

The Case of Niels Abel

by David Shavin

July 16—China has put on the table the beautiful—and very 'American'—mission of wiping out poverty by the year 2030.

The type of thinking required today to finally wipe out poverty, disease and hunger will involve a level of creativity once described by Lyndon LaRouche as being able to "play ping-pong with the stars."

The beautiful composition of a new alliance of nations pushing the frontiers of plasma physics, fusion technologies and materials processing, as the surplus is deployed to craft massive infrastructure projects throughout the developing world, requires a level of thinking and emotional development that will make future generations stand in awe.[1]

This type of thinking is that of the 'poet-mathematician'. It was also expressed in Plato's **Republic** *as a 'philosopher-king'—the almost impossible, but completely necessary development of leaders, who pursue the most difficult paradoxes in astronomy and music, so*

Niels Abel

as to harmonize their souls with the complexities of the development of human communities. After the American Revolution, a youthful genius, Karl Gauss, in what was apparently an obscure mathematical text, went boldly where most others feared to tread. An identifiable, small core of youth, took up Gauss' challenge. In the United States Edgar Alan Poe popularized the 'poet-mathematician' in the 1840's with his 'Dupin' character, who was based on one of those youth.

This report will develop the case of Niels Abel, one of Gauss' youth generation.

Introduction

First, pick any number, that is, a positive, integral number. Let's try, for example, 23. Multiply it by 9. We'll get 207. Then, add up all the digits in the product, $2 + 0 + 7$. You'll always get 9, regardless of what number you start with.[2] This is not magic. It has to do with a type of brainwashing you went through in first grade. It is not difficult to discover why this works nor how you were brainwashed; but, for maximum therapeutic benefit, we'll leave this exercise to the reader. This simple example is only a drop in Karl Friedrich Gauss' ocean, but it introduces an overlooked capacity. The human

---

1. See LaRouche's Four Laws: http://www.larouchepub.com/lar/2016/4329_revisit_4_laws.html. In particular, "The creation of credit… must be assured … to create a general economic recovery of the nation, per capita, and for rate of net effects in productivity …. This means intrinsically, a thoroughly scientific, rather than a merely mathematical one, and by the related increase of the effective energy-flux density per capita, and for the human population when considered as each and all as a whole. The ceaseless increase of the physical-productivity of employment …" is key. "Man is mankind's only true measure of the history of our Solar system, and what reposes within it."

2. In the cases where you get a sum larger than 10, repeat the adding of digits—e.g., 11 multiplied by 9 yields 99; and adding $9 + 9$ yields 18, not 9. Here, adding the $1 + 8$ will, once again, yield 9.

mind, forms patterns and organizes the world of which it is itself an integral part; though marvelous, it is not magical.

Next, a simple poetic snapshot: *"From fairest creatures, we desire increase . . . ."*

Which is the verb? Does beauty impel us to desire increase, or does it increase our desire?

Did Shakespeare's beautiful command of language change us, and, make us, as personalities, more than we were? Or did it make us fall in love with the bard, increasing our thirst for his poetic power?

Clearly, Shakespeare crafted an opening theme to his "Sonnets" where both 'desire' and 'increase' function as verbs, exploiting a world where the (subjective) beauty and (objective) truth share a fruitful interplay. If the world is constructed in such a rich fashion, it behooves us to raise our thought-processes and language up to the level of what we're investigating—rather than reducing it to what appears easiest to deal with.

The poet has an ability to seize upon, and play upon, powerful capacities of the mind, dramatically expanding the power of the culture's overall mental activity.

Lyndon LaRouche's passion for, and rigorous development of, the mind's unique and necessary capacity for transforming the world, is at the core of his rejection of formalist mathematics and his insistence upon the role of what is called here the 'poet-mathematician'.[3] The term, 'poet-mathematician', itself, is a healthy juxtaposition. The jarring aspect of setting 'poet' in combination with 'mathematician' aids in opening up critical areas of investigation. It would help to approximate the subject with another juxtaposition: The world objectively requires national banking, non-magical national banking; and only a fool would attempt to carry out national banking without the capacities of the poet-mathematician.

I. Measuring World-Changing Power

In 1801, the young genius, Carl Friedrich Gauss, published a stunningly powerful poetic work in a most austere form, entitled *Disquisitiones Arithmeticae*. He boldly announced, from the mountaintop, the laws and powers of mind behind the properties of number. The harmonic interplay of the exponents, bases and residue, developed in Gauss' *Disquisitiones Arithmeticae*, bore many fruits and a vast amount of implications. But one fundamental, and identifiable, and rather general principle concerns us here: The conjoined measurement of both

a) the internally-generated power to grow, captured in the exponentials, and

b) the externally-generated 'accretion'-type of growth, or, actually, the magnitude of the resultant activity after a cycle of production.

That is: Not to measure exponential and arithmetic growth separately, but to take a measure of their interplay, a more complex and inter-connected process.

Gauss' arithmetic-geometric mean is one simple case of this type of interplay. The arithmetic mean (AM) is what most people understand as the 'average' of two numbers. Half-way between 2 and 8 is 5. The geometric mean (GM) involves the internally-generated 'exponential' growth. In growing from 2 to 8, the 'half-way' point is 4; that is, 2 doubles to 4, and repeating this 'doubling'-growth, doubles to 8. One can determine this geometric 'half-way' point by multiplying the beginning and end points of the growth (2x8=16), and then figuring out the magnitude that acts upon itself to

painted by Christian Albrecht Jensen

Johann Carl Friedrich Gauss
(1777-1855)

---

3. See, e.g., LaRouche's "Poetry Must Begin to Supercede Mathematics in Physics."

portrait by Auguste Eugene Leray
Sophie Germain

Johann Peter Gustav Lejeune Dirichlet

Évariste Galois

Bernhard Riemann

obtain the same result (that is, what is usually called, taking the square-root of 16 yields 4). A geometric 'root' really is something that grows differently than, e.g., arithmetically stacking bricks in a pile. Gauss develops the arithmetic-geometric mean, whereby one successively takes the arithmetic and geometric means of the former arithmetic and geometric means. (That is, e.g., going from 2 to 8, the GM is 4, the AM is 5; then, next stage, between 4 and 5, the GM is the root of 20, and the AM is the slightly larger 4.5. The two limits converge towards each other with some rapidity to form the arithmetic-geometric mean.

Is this a silly game, designed to keep math majors busy? What physical significance would an arithmetic-geometric mean have? Put a bit too simply, the geometric is where one measures the power of a process (e.g., whether it grows 'fully acting upon itself,' squaring itself); and the arithmetic, where there is some significance to quantifying how much has been produced at the end of a production cycle. We have power being measured relative to a specific moment in the production process. If it is a physical process worth encouraging, it will be fruitful in some fashion. That fruitfulness has physically changed the world. That physical process, after one cycle of production, is now acting upon a different magnitude. The dynamics of bodies moving in elliptical orbits, or the dynamics of an integrated manufacturing facility, require physically-driven measurements—frequently at variance with the 'back-engineering', or ass-backwards engineering involved in someone calculating 'how much profit will my money make?'.

Here, power acts, producing a different world than before, changing what that power can accomplish in the next production cycle. Here, a language has to be developed to capture the historically-specific actions of power, or '*dunamis*'.[4] Lawfully, and somewhat ironically, the individuals who most seriously, most passionately, took up this mission, have proven to be, as rather unique individuals, the most fascinating exemplars, in their own personalities, of the higher-ordered mathematics. The historically-specific realities of their lives, rise to a level beyond mere biographical side-notes, a level helpful in delineating how they were able to develop such a rigorous and higher-ordered language, appropriate for mapping how the mind intervenes upon the outside world.

The most serious students of Gauss' *Disquisitiones Arithmeticae*, his 'poet-mathematicians', were Sophie Germain, LeJeune Dirichlet,[5] Niels Abel, Evariste Galois, and Bernhard Riemann. Common to all five is that their actual activities and methods of thinking, always combined two critical components:

1) a non-'mathematical', musical and/or poetic core; and

2) an identifiable, historically-specific moral core—where it is clear that the strength and power in their conceptions and dealings with matters of 'discreteness'/'continuity', revolve around each individual's courageous decision to deal with nothing short

---

4. Power/'dunamis' is developed by Bruce Director in "Riemann for Anti-Dummies: Part 33" : Hyperbolic Functions—A Fugue Across 25 Centuries; see also: "Riemann for Anti-Dummies: Part 66"

5. The case of Dirichlet involves the author's development of the role of the German-Jewish Mendelssohn family. See: Philosophical Vignettes from the Political Life of Moses Mendelssohn, *Fidelio*, Vol. 8, No. 2, Summer, 1999, and for the Dirichlet case: "Rebecca Dirichlet's Development Of the Complex Domain, *EIR*, June 11, 2010.

C. Schulin

Potsdamer Bahnhof in Berlin.

of the totality of the universe.

That is, they themselves, personally, are located as an exemplar of discreteness in the continuity of the processes of the universe.

Here, we shall examine the case of Gauss' Norwegian protégé, Niels Abel—and, in particular, his wonderfully strange year on the way to Paris, when Abel's unique aesthetic education empowered him to push forward the measurement of the mind's activity upon the world.

August Leopold Crelle

development of his power of inversion, which he would later apply to his so-called mathematical work. As Abel put it: "One learns many strange Things on such a Tour, Things of which I can find more use than if I were purely studying Mathematics."

Berlin and the Composer-Mathematician

First, in Berlin, in the fall of 1825, he met August Crelle, a man primarily known today, if at all, only for the mathematical periodical he founded, "Crelle's Journal." Crelle greatly valued Abel's talent and honesty from their first meeting: Crelle discussed one of his own mathematical papers—and, evidently, Abel was able to quickly explain where Crelle had fallen short. Abel was pleasantly shocked in finding that Crelle's Monday night gatherings were not mathematics seminars, but rather *musikabends*! Abel begins his description of Crelle's gathering: "There is at his place some kind of meeting where music is mainly discussed, of which unfortunately I do not understand much." Up to that point, Abel's passion for the theater had been more advanced than for the concert stage.

Crelle's primary job was to develop transportation for the Prussian state, whereby he would create the first Prussian railroad, that from Berlin to Potsdam. But he also composed music, including settings of Johann Wolfgang von Goethe and Friedrich Schiller.[6] He had authored a work on music in

---

II. Abel's Wonderfully Strange Year

Niels Abel was a talented Norwegian youth who, at eighteen, had already devoured Gauss' *Disquisitiones Arithmeticae*. He had set himself the task of developing Gauss' treatment of the elliptical transcendentals and such curves as the *lemniscates*. However, it wasn't until he turned twenty-three that he was able to travel to Paris, via Berlin, Leipzig, Prague and Vienna, to test himself at the centers of learning and study. Though largely overlooked by historians and biographers, Abel's aesthetic education is in full view. One particular core of his aesthetic education had to do with the

---

6. Crelle's *Zehn Gesänge am Fortepiano* (op. 3) seem to be from the period of the Liberation War (1813/14). The ten settings, in order, are: C. A. Tiedge's *Abendfeier*; Goethe's *Der untreue Knabe*; *Liebe*; Bechtolsheim's *Die Blume aus Norden*; Goethe's *Der Fischer*; *Mein Edmund*; A. H. Niemeyer's *Dreistimmiger Kanon*; Friedrich von Matthisson's *Elysium*; Friedrich von Hardenberg's *Sängers Klage*; and Goethe's *Rastlose Liebe*. He also set Goethe's *Neue Liebe, neues Leben* and Hardenberg's *Zulima*.

Felix Mendelssohn

Sara Levy

1823, and on December 5, 1824, he gave a memorial lecture, on the occasion of the anniversary of Mozart's death. For this occasion, he arranged for a performance of Mozart's *Requiem* which included the fifteen year-old Felix Mendelssohn, who served as the orchestra. Crelle also had longstanding connections and activities with the Berlin *Singakademie,* including its director, Carl Friedrich Zelter, and its chief supporter, Sara Levy. (Zelter was Mendelssohn's teacher and Sara Levy was the aunt of Mendelssohn's mother.)

It is not known specifically what Crelle's Monday evening music seminars studied; however a decent hypothesis may be ventured. At this very time of Abel's visit (1825), a special work had been dedicated to Crelle: a piano-arrangement of Mozart's (K. 546) *Adagio and Fugue* quartet-study of Bach's "Musical Offering."[7] It is not a big stretch to assume that this work played a central role in Crelle's seminar that year. The arranger, J. P. Schmidt, the same Winter that Abel was in Berlin, published Beethoven's Op. 29 String Quintet, arranged for four hands[8] and dedicated to the teenagers, Fanny and Felix Mendelssohn—drawing the circle even tighter. (Perhaps, the only question left seems to be whether Fanny and Felix performed this work at Crelle's, at their great-aunt's— Sara Levy's—or at both locations!) That Felix, within months, produced his own first string quintet, again points to the likelihood that these specific works were indeed part and parcel of the social discussions of these circles.

Abel may not have understood much about musical discussions when he first arrived, but Crelle certainly seems to have had other plans for him. He introduced Abel to the Mendelssohns' circle by getting him invited to Sara Levy's Saturday evening *musikabends.* Crelle had known Levy over the previous two decades from the Berlin *Singakademie.* Briefly, regarding Sara: she was a student of Bach's eldest son, Wilhelm Friedrich; she was the prime source for Bach manuscripts; and was the piano soloist performing from her Bach manuscripts with the *Singakademie.* Finally, it was her manuscript copy of J. S. Bach's "St. Matthew's Passion," given to her great-nephew, Felix, that occasioned the historic 1829 Bach Renaissance[9]—which played such an important role for Felix Mendelssohn's soon-to-be brother-in-law, LeJeune Dirichlet.

So, Abel's weekly schedule in Berlin is known to have included: Monday night *musikabend*s at Crelle's; discussions on Gauss on Friday mid-day walks with Crelle and Jakob Steiner; and Saturday evening *musikabend*s at Sara Levy's. In all, during his famous 'trip to Paris', Abel would actually spend fully one-half of his time in Berlin with Crelle and Sarah Levy. Crelle's famous journal itself is a residue of Abel's stopover in Berlin, as it was founded in the wake of Abel's visit, and its initial issues were centered upon Abel's works. (Later, Crelle tried to get Abel to become the editor of the journal.) Before leaving Berlin for Paris, one of Crelle's mathematicians, Professor Dirksen, provided Abel with a letter of recommendation, introducing him

---

7. *Adagio and Fugue*, K. 546, arranged, *La Fugue quatuor de W.A. Mozart arrangée pour le Piano=Forte à quatre mains et dédiée à Monsieur Crelle par son ami J.P. Schmidt.* Trautwein: Berlin, [1825].

8. Beethoven's String Quintet, Op. 29, arranged, *Rondeau, tiré du Grand Quintuor, Oeuvre 29, Arrangé pour le Pianoforte à quatre mains et dedié à Mdmlle Fanny & Msr. Felix Mendelssohn-Bartholdy par J.P. Schmidt.*

9. "Rebecca Dirichlet's Development Of the Complex Domain," *EIR*, June 11, 2010, pp 31-32.

to Alexander von Humboldt. Of some note, Crelle and Dirksen were well aware that Humboldt was recruiting talented geniuses to help build up Berlin.

Bach, Freiburg and Crystallography

Next, on Feb. 22, 1826, Abel goes for a month's-long stay in Leipzig and Freiburg, where he works, primarily, with the Naumanns—sons of the Dresden composer, Johann Gottlieb Naumann. The father had studied Bach's "Preludes and Fugues" with one of Bach's Leipzig students, Gottfried August Homilius. Naumann had composed for Benjamin Franklin's Glass-harmonica (1786), and had been involved with Schiller's friend, Christian Gottfried Körner, in the drive for a national theater.

Exhibit in the Freiberg Mining Museum.

Abel, along with his Norwegian traveling companion, Baltazar Mathias Keilhau, first met, in Leipzig, with the composer's son, K. F. Naumann.[10] This Naumann had recently visited Norway's mountains to study crystals, and had just finished translating Keilhau's geology work from Norwegian into German. Within months of their meeting, Naumann would become the professor of crystallography at Freiburg, studying the exceptions to perfect symmetry in crystals (e.g., distortion of axes, twinning, and chiralitry or 'handedness'). Naumann called them *enantio-morphisms*. After two days in Leipzig, they—Abel and Kielhau—are off to Freiburg, where K. F.'s brother, August Naumann, taught mathematics. Abel meets August at a mineralogy seminar, and spends significant time with him over the next month. The Leipzig/Freiburg discussions might have touched upon mathematics, but evidently only as an adjunct to the paradigmatic cases of the crystalline exceptions to perfect symmetry—a key feature of Abel's mathematical developments. Abel writes of August: "a really gifted fellow" and "a very agreeable man and we associated harmoniously . . . ."

The trips to Leipzig and Freiburg were, somehow, not part of the official agenda. Abel had been expected to bee-line toward Paris, where the mathematical elite were said to reside. Abel's teacher at Christiania University, Christopher Hansteen—himself an important part of Gauss' geo-magnetic project—commented upon Abel's 'diversion' away from Paris: "...[W]hy that young god Thor, searching for his hammer, wants to swing to Leipzig and surroundings I do not know . . . . [Regardless, he] always arrives where he is supposed to, even if he does not move straight to it." Abel's response to Hansteen is telling: "...[T]here will be no lack of ideas for several years. I shall probably gather more on my travels, for just at present there are many thoughts circulating in my head." With Bach-ian inversions and transformations, Mozart's study of Bach, and the implications of the dissymmetry of physical transformations of nature, there should be little wonder! While Abel's powerful methods of

a) inversion—of reversing investigations, from 'what we may infer from the facts' to 'what must be the case for functions to work at all'—and

b) isolating the non-symmetric characteristics of a system, might have been suggested earlier by some of the procedures of Abel's earlier teacher, Bernt Holmboe, and his university professor Hansteen, it was given courage and shape in Berlin, Leipzig, and Freiburg.

---

10. The composer-father had actually given "K. F." four names, notably including "Amadeus"—this five years after Mozart's death.

Library of Congress

Edgar Allan Poe

Frédéric Thjéodore Lix

C. Auguste Dupin, from an illustration for The Purloined Letter *by Edgar Allan Poe.*

The 23-year-old Abel now describes to Hansteen his newly-formulated plan to put analysis on a rigorous basis, from the top down: "Everywhere [in advanced analysis, especially the tradition of Euler] one finds this miserable way of concluding from the special to the general, and it is extremely peculiar that such a procedure has led to so few of the so-called paradoxes. [For Abel, the so-called paradoxes are to be sought!] It is really interesting to seek the cause. To my mind it lies in the fact that in analysis, one is largely occupied with functions which can be expressed by powers. As soon as other functions enter—this, however, is not often the case—then it does not work any more and a number of connected, incorrect theorems arise from the false conclusions. … It works out satisfactorily as long as one proceeds generally. …" This is a pretty strong echo of Leibniz's "analysis situs" approach (also characterized by LaRouche as a "top-down" approach—to be preferred to that of the "bottoms-up").

The 'Melancholy Spectre' of Venice

Abel's visit to Venice provided him a *'Feindbild,'* an enemy-image, for his moral objection to 'mathematics-by-induction.' Abel's description: "There is a melancholy Spectre invading Venice. Everywhere one sees Signs of former Glory and contemporary Wretchedness. …Everything testifies to Decay." The state of

mathematics, in not openly developing the implications of the *Disquisitiones*, was also one with "signs of former glory and contemporary wretchedness." This should not be discounted as simply a 'poetic truth.' The backward state of build-from-the-bottom mathematics (what Poe would call, in honor of Francis Bacon, 'Hoggism') was not merely wasteful; it never had to happen. Its very existence betrayed a systemic problem, not to be overlooked. For Abel, the very fact that there had been a Venice, a second incarnation of Rome, could not be accepted as a necessary feature of the world—without suffering the penalty of mental damage to one's own faculties! Even this part of his aesthetical education would prove of significant utility in his upcoming dealings with the mathematical reactionaries of Paris.

Otherwise of note, in between Freiburg and Venice, Abel saw an Italian opera in Dresden, and Schiller's "William Tell" in Prague. In Prague, he also sought out the heads of the astronomical observatory. (It might be imagined that Abel benefitted from discussions with those working at what was once Johann Kepler's observatory, but, unfortunately, this author has not been able to develop a case for reconstructing those discussions.) Then, after Venice, his last major stop before Paris was a six-week stay in Vienna, which included visits to theaters and discussions with Crelle's friend, J. J. Edler von Littrow, the director of the Vienna Observatory.[11] Littrow provided Abel with what would be a critical letter of introduction to the director of the Paris observatory, Alexis Bouvard.

Paris: Abel Links Up with Dirichlet, His Fellow 'Countryman' in the Land of the *Disquisitiones*

Bouvard introduced Abel to a key group of French republicans around Audebart, Baron de Férrusac. In 1823, Audebart had established what would later be called the *Bulletin General et Universel de Sciences et de l'Industrie,* which reported useful scientific advances to Parisians, especially those from outside of Paris. Audebart's journal was given a favorable review by one member of the French Academy, C. August Dupin—the actual scientist whose name Edgar Alan Poe would use for his fictional poet-mathematician! Audebart's editor, J. F. Saigey, employed Abel to write short synopses of articles from other science journals. Abel's first submissions included an account of his own proof on the impossibility of the quintic,[12] along with an account of his Norwegian article on the moon's gravitational effect on the pendulum.

Audebart's scientific library, maintained by Saigey, was the gathering place for the serious thinkers in Paris, for those who would not be hemmed in by Augustin-Louis Cauchy and by the Restorationist grip over the Academy. (From the 1815 Congress of Vienna until the 1830 July Revolution, France was administered under the restored monarchies of Louis XVI's two brothers, and Cauchy was their controller at the Academy.) It was there, at Saigey's library, that Abel met with Lejeune Dirichlet, who, at 21, was three years Abel's junior. It is certainly possible that Dirichlet had sought out Abel, due to his published account of the quintic. Abel writes (10/24/1826) of Dirichlet: "He is a very sharp Mathematician... [H]e has shown

the impossibility of solving in whole Numbers the [quintic] equation $x^5 + y^5 = z^5$ and other neat Things." He made sure to record: "Herrn Le-jeune Dirichlet, a Prussian, who the other Day came to me and said he regarded me his Countryman." Dirichlet certainly was not confused: he knew he was talking with a Norwegian! While he might have been referring to Abel's time in Berlin and possibly even the Humboldt plan to recruit Abel to Berlin, it were very likely, knowing Dirichlet, that he bonded with Abel in the 'country of the *Disquisitiones.'*

Dealing with Demons—LaPlace and Cauchy

This July-October 1826 period in Paris saw Abel's perhaps most concentrated work, centered around his paper on transcendental functions. That work should be viewed as the fruit, in particular, of Berlin, Leipzig, and Freiburg. The introduction of his *Mémoire sur une propriété générale d'une classe trés étendue des functions transcendantes* was read by Joseph Fourier before the Academy on October 30, and then given to Augustin-Louis Cauchy to make a report. Abel had described his powerful 'inversion' plan of attack, as formulated back in Freiburg. His methods allowed for a breath-taking expansion of the human race's ability to deal with transcendental functions, where exponential and logarithmic functions did not lead up to, but rather were derived from the elliptic and higher transcendentals. Higher species of curves, of characteristic actions that accounted for all the important features of the visible curves, were made subject to human culture and deliberation. Cauchy promptly buried the report.

Prior to October 30th, Abel had offered Cauchy time to examine the *Mémoire.* "I showed it to Mr Cauchy, but he scarcely deigned to glance at it." After the presentation of the paper to the Academy, *The Memoir on Transcendental Functions* disappeared, with no report being produced. Cauchy claimed that he simply lost the paper. Even for someone committed to suppressing scientific development and suppressing genius, it was a rather brutal and desperate action. Still, Abel might not have been completely surprised. In his preceding three months in Paris, Abel had already described the problem: "Cauchy is *'fou'* [mad] and there is Nothing to come out of him, although he is the mathematician for the present Time who knows how Mathematics ought to be treated. His Issues are excellent, but

---

11. For what it is worth, the "Littrow projection" is said to be the only conformal retro-azimuthal map projection. Curiously, Littrow's own 'academic advisor' back in Prague had been August Gottlieb Meissner, the professor of aesthetics and classical literature—who happens to be the source for the story that the Venetian agent, Casanova, had tried to intervene upon Mozart's "Don Giovanni" production back in 1787.

12. Algorithmic solutions had been found for 2nd, 3rd and 4th -power equations. (Algebra students typically learn the simplest one, the "quadratic equation.") Contrary to expectations from the 'bottoms-up' crowd, not only was no such algorithm discovered for 5th-power equations, but Abel, and Dirichlet, had addressed why such was the case, proving no such algorithm was possible.

Augustin-Louis Cauchy

Jean-Baptiste Paulin Guérin

*Pierre Simon Marquis de Laplace
(1745-1827)*

he writes very obscurely. … Cauchy is tremendously Catholic and a bigot. A sorely strange Thing for a Mathematician." What is this "sorely strange Thing"? A mathematician capable enough to identify the leading mathematical issues, but who has chosen to obscure and smother them. Abel's analytical ability, in identifying the characteristic evil in the scientific community of 1826, clearly stemmed from his moral commitment to truth-seeking, and his moral repulsion for the 'Venetian decay' disease.

Further, Abel recorded his analysis as to why the disease would not be easily cured in Paris. He was convinced that the older generation around the Academy would not challenge Cauchy. The 74-year-old Adrien-Marie Legendre was an "exceedingly obliging Man but unhappily as old as a Stone." Sylvestre François Lacroix, though, biologically, only sixty, was "awfully skaldic [ancient, from the Middle Ages] and remarkably Old," while Simeon Denis Poisson was "somewhat captivated by himself." But Abel was especially exercised over the sophistical Pierre-Simon LaPlace: "He appears quick and small, but He has the same Shortcoming of which [the demon] Haltefanden accuses Zambullo;[13] that is to say, *la mauvaise habitude de couper la langue de gens'.*" ['He has the horrible habit of silencing people'.] Abel certainly recognized that LaPlace's deterministic axiomatics left him with

the felt need to invoke a hypothesized 'superior intelligence,' LaPlace's Demon, which demon would pre-determine everything mechanistically—a ruse little different from the "Invisible Hand." Such sophistries were designed to cover over, rather than reveals—not unlike the obscurantism that Abel objected to in LaPlace's collaborator, Cauchy … an obscurantism which would now extend to simply burying Abel's masterpiece.

Abel's ability to forge ahead, in the face of the reactionary social culture of Restorationist mathematics in Cauchy's Paris, had everything to do with his previous year in Berlin, Leipzig, Freiburg, Prague and Vienna—and, yes, even decadent Venice. Recall Abel's forecast: "One learns many strange Things on such a Tour, Things of which I can find more use than if I were purely studying Mathematics." The full facets of Abel's creative personality found lawful expression in Bach; in the powerful language of inversion; and of dissymmetric, characteristic processes in crystallography. The development of access to higher-order causal processes cannot but give form and shape to the previously hidden processes of the 'mathematician'. (And these hidden processes even apply to the first-grade mathematician, in his or her unthinking acceptance of the number 'ten'.)[14]

---

13. The two are characters from a topical fictional work by Lesage.

14. For the attentive, here is one explanation of the number puzzle from the top of the article, for the reader to compare with his or her own solution: The key is '9' as the last numeral of the 'base 10' system. Multiplying by nine creates a series: 9, 18, 27, 36, 45, 54, 63, 72, 81, 90, 99, 108, etc. Each addition of 9 lowers the digit column by 1 and increases the next column to the left by 1. This 'hidden' property is simply a function of the intervention made by your first-grade teacher, who halted the enumeration of numbers at 9, and then spent some weeks, drilling and grilling you on the importance of the columns and the place-holder role of zero. (It was very important to line up your columns when adding.) There is no problem in ordering numbers in groups of ten, with columns representing increased powers. The problem only arises when the mind is deceived as to how the action of shaping 'number-space' has implications.

III. Those Who Already Have the Death of Abel on Their Consciences

Abel received no response in Paris to his opus magnum, locked away in Cauchy's study. He wrote home about the ostracism: "On the whole, I do not like the French as well as the Germans; the French are extremely reserved toward strangers. It is very difficult to become closely associated with them, and I dare not hope for it. Everybody works for himself without concern for others. All want to instruct, and nobody wants to learn. The most absolute egotism reigns supreme." Years of intellectual fascism had taken its toll around the Academy. Then his "Countryman" Dirichlet left Paris; Alexander Humboldt had arranged a professorship in Germany for Dirichlet. From November, 1826 until January, 1827, Abel's last three months in Paris, he was increasingly isolated. It seems likely that this is the precise period when Abel contracted tuberculosis, which was then the equivalent of a death sentence. His actions indicate that his prime concern was to get home and to concentrate on his own work for whatever time he had left. Though he did take the next four months to revisit Berlin, attending the *musikabend*s at Crelle's and at Sara Levy's, he surprised Crelle by turning down his offer to become the editor of *Crelle's Journal*. When he left for home, he had less than two years remaining.

Crelle, probably in 1828, wrote Humboldt: "The gentlemen Dirichlet, Abel, Jacobi, and Steiner, who all, except Abel, already are in the service of the Prussian government, represent in reality a group of young mathematicians giving the greatest expectations for the advance of science. Perhaps they, in time, will become mathematicians of the very highest rank, for in spite of their youth, science already owes essential progress to them… Again the Prussian government is in a position to support talents so great that nature only rarely produces them. For this science will be in a debt of gratitude to your Excellency." Crelle and Humboldt still planned to get Abel a professorship in Berlin. In April, 1829, Crelle's letter arrived, with the news that Abel had received his appointment in Berlin. However, Neils Abel had died, only days earlier.

Karl Jacobi, Abel's closest mathematical collabo-

Wilhelm von Humboldt

rator in Berlin, who had walked with Crelle and Abel every Friday, would exert pressure upon the Paris Academy to produce Abel's "lost" manuscript. With intervention from the Norwegian consul in Paris, Cauchy eventually succeeded in locating Abel's manuscript—but not before he had succeeded, again, in "losing" the manuscript submitted to the Academy of the next-in-line of Gauss' geniuses, that of Evariste Galois. In December 1831, from a prison in Paris, the precocious genius, Galois wrote: "I must tell you how manuscripts go astray in the portfolios of the members of the Institute, although I cannot in truth conceive of such carelessness on the part of those who already have the death of Abel on their consciences."

The case of Galois underlines and intensifies that of Abel. But in both cases, to repeat from above: "…their actual activities and methods of thinking always combined two critical components:

1. A non-'mathematical' musical and/or poetic core; and

2. An identifiable, historically-specific moral core—where it is clear that the strength and power in their conceptions and dealings with matters of 'discreteness'/'continuity,' revolve around the individual's courageous decision to deal with nothing short of the totality of the universe. That is, they themselves, personally, are located as an exemplar of discreteness in the continuity of the processes of the universe."

III. The Fraud of 'Russia-Gate' Exposed

MEMORANDUM FOR: The President
FROM: Veteran Intelligence Professionals for Sanity (VIPS)
SUBJECT: Was the "Russian Hack" an Inside Job?

Executive Summary

Forensic studies of "Russian hacking" into Democratic National Committee computers last year reveal that on July 5, 2016, data was **leaked (not hacked)** by a person with physical access to DNC computers, and then doctored to incriminate Russia.

After examining metadata from the "Guccifer 2.0" July 5, 2016 intrusion into the DNC server, independent cyber investigators have concluded that an insider copied DNC data onto an external storage device, and that "telltale signs" implicating Russia were then inserted.

Key among the findings of the independent forensic investigations is the conclusion that the DNC data was copied onto a storage device **at a speed that far exceeds an Internet capability for a remote hack**. Of equal importance, the forensics show that the copying and doctoring were performed on the East coast of the U.S. Thus far, mainstream media have ignored the findings of these independent studies [see here and here].

Independent analyst Skip Folden, a retired IBM Program Manager for Information Technology US, who examined the recent forensic findings, is a co-author of this Memorandum. He has drafted a more detailed technical report titled "Cyber-Forensic Investigation of 'Russian Hack' and Missing Intelligence Community Disclaimers," and sent it to the of-fices of the Special Counsel and the Attorney General. VIPS member William Binney, a former Technical Director at the National Security Agency, and other senior NSA "alumni" in VIPS attest to the professionalism of the independent forensic findings.

The recent forensic studies fill in a critical gap. Why the FBI neglected to perform any independent forensics on the original "Guccifer 2.0" material remains a mystery—as does the lack of any sign that the "hand-picked analysts" from the FBI, CIA, and NSA, who wrote the "Intelligence Community Assessment" dated January 6, 2017, gave any attention to forensics.

NOTE: There has been so much conflation of charges about hacking that we wish to make very clear the pri-

Director of National Intelligence James Clapper (right) talks with President Barack Obama in the Oval Office, with John Brennan and other national security aides present.

mary focus of this Memorandum. We focus specifically on the July 5, 2016 alleged Guccifer 2.0 "hack" of the DNC server. In earlier VIPS memoranda we addressed the lack of any evidence connecting the Guccifer 2.0 alleged hacks and WikiLeaks, and we asked President Obama specifically to disclose any evidence that WikiLeaks received DNC data from the Russians [see here and here].

Addressing this point at his last press conference (January 18), he described "the conclusions of the intelligence community" as "not conclusive," even though the Intelligence Community Assessment of January 6 expressed "high confidence" that Russian intelligence "relayed material it acquired from the DNC . . . to WikiLeaks."

Obama's admission came as no surprise to us. It has long been clear to us that the reason the U.S. government lacks conclusive evidence of a transfer of a "Russian hack" to WikiLeaks is because there was no such transfer. Based mostly on the cumulatively unique technical experience of our ex-NSA colleagues, we have been saying for almost a year that the DNC data reached WikiLeaks via a copy/leak by a DNC insider (but almost certainly not the same person who copied DNC data on July 5, 2016).

From the information available, we conclude that the same inside-DNC, copy/leak process was used at two different times, by two different entities, for two distinctly different purposes:

(1) an inside leak to WikiLeaks before Julian Assange announced on June 12, 2016, that he had DNC documents and planned to publish them (which he did on July 22)—the presumed objective being to expose strong DNC bias toward the Clinton candidacy; and

(2) a separate leak on July 5, 2016, to pre-emptively taint anything WikiLeaks might later publish by "showing" it came from a "Russian hack."

* * *

Mr. President:

This is our first VIPS Memorandum for you, but we have a history of letting U.S. Presidents know when we think our former intelligence colleagues have gotten something important wrong, and why. For

UN photo/Sophia Paris

Secretary of State Colin Powell addressed the United Nations on Feb. 5, 2003, citing satellite photos which supposedly proved that Iraq had WMD, but the evidence proved bogus.

example, our first such memorandum, a same-day commentary for President George W. Bush on Colin Powell's U.N. speech on February 5, 2003, warned that the "unintended consequences were likely to be catastrophic," should the U.S. attack Iraq and "justfy" the war on intelligence that we retired intelligence officers could readily see as fraudulent and driven by a war agenda.

The January 6 "Intelligence Community Assessment" by "hand-picked" analysts from the FBI, CIA, and NSA seems to fit into the same agenda-driven category. It is largely based on an "assessment," not supported by any apparent evidence, that a shadowy entity with the moniker "Guccifer 2.0" hacked the DNC on behalf of Russian intelligence and gave DNC emails to WikiLeaks.

The recent forensic findings mentioned above have put a huge dent in that assessment and cast serious doubt on the underpinnings of the extraordinarily successful campaign to blame the Russian government for hacking. The pundits and politicians who have led the charge against Russian "meddling" in the U.S. election can be expected to try to cast doubt on the forensic findings, if they ever do bubble up into the mainstream media. But the principles of physics don't lie; and the technical limitations of today's Internet are widely understood. We are prepared to answer any substantive challenges on their merits.

You may wish to ask CIA Director Mike Pompeo

what he knows about this. Our own lengthy intelligence community experience suggests that it is possible that neither former CIA Director John Brennan, nor the cyber-warriors who worked for him, have been completely candid with their new director regarding how this all went down.

Copied, Not Hacked

As indicated above, the independent forensic work just completed focused on data *copied (not hacked)* by a shadowy persona named "Guccifer 2.0." The forensics reflect what seems to have been a desperate effort to "blame the Russians" for publishing highly embarrassing DNC emails three days before the Democratic convention last July. Since the content of the DNC emails reeked of pro-Clinton bias, her campaign saw an overriding need to divert attention from content to provenance—as in, who "hacked" those DNC emails? The campaign was enthusiastically supported by a compliant "mainstream" media; they are still on a roll.

"The Russians" were the ideal culprit. And, after WikiLeaks editor Julian Assange announced on June 12, 2016, "We have emails related to Hillary Clinton which are pending publication," her campaign had more than a month before the convention to insert its own "forensic facts" and prime the media pump to put the blame on "Russian meddling." Mrs. Clinton's PR chief Jennifer Palmieri has explained how she used golf carts to make the rounds at the convention. She wrote that her "mission was to get the press to focus on something even we found difficult to process: the prospect that Russia had not only hacked and stolen emails from the DNC, but that it had done so to help Donald Trump and hurt Hillary Clinton."

Independent cyber-investigators have now completed the kind of forensic work that the intelligence assessment did not do. Oddly, the "hand-picked" intelligence analysts contented themselves with "assessing" this and "assessing" that. In contrast, the investigators dug deep and came up with verifiable evidence from

Democratic presidential nominee Hillary Clinton at the third debate with Republican nominee Donald Trump.

metadata found in the record of the alleged Russian hack.

They found that the purported "hack" of the DNC by Guccifer 2.0 was not a hack, by Russia or anyone else. Rather it originated with a copy (onto an external storage device—a thumb drive, for example) by an insider. The data was leaked after being doctored with a cut-and-paste job to implicate Russia. We do not know who or what the murky Guccifer 2.0 is. You may wish to ask the FBI.

The Time Sequence

June 12, 2016: Assange announces WikiLeaks is about to publish "emails related to Hillary Clinton."

June 15, 2016: DNC contractor CrowdStrike, (with a dubious professional record and multiple conflicts of interest) announces that malware has been found on the DNC server and claims there is evidence it was injected by Russians.

June 15, 2016: On the same day, "Guccifer 2.0" affirms the DNC statement; claims responsibility for the "hack"; claims to be a WikiLeaks source; and posts a document that the forensics show was synthetically tainted with "Russian fingerprints."

We do not think that the June 12 & 15 timing was pure coincidence. Rather, it suggests the start of a preemptive move to associate Russia with anything WikiLeaks might have been about to publish and to "show" that it came from a Russian hack.

The Key Event

July 5, 2016: In the early evening, Eastern Daylight Time, someone working in the EDT time zone with a computer directly connected to the DNC server or DNC Local Area Network, copied 1,976 MegaBytes of data in 87 seconds onto an external storage device. **That speed is many times faster than what is physically possible with a hack.**

It thus appears that the purported "hack" of the DNC by Guccifer 2.0 (the self-proclaimed WikiLeaks source) was not a hack by Russia or anyone else, but was rather a copy of DNC data onto an external storage device. Moreover, the forensics performed on the metadata reveal there was a subsequent synthetic insertion—a cut-and-paste job using a Russian template, with the clear aim of attributing the data to a "Russian hack." This was all performed in the East Coast time zone.

WikiLeaks founder Julian Assange.

cc/David G. Silvers

'Obfuscation & De-obfuscation'

Mr. President, the disclosure described below may be related. Even if it is not, it is something we think you should be made aware of in this general connection. On March 7, 2017, WikiLeaks began to publish a trove of original CIA documents that WikiLeaks labeled "Vault 7." WikiLeaks said it got the trove from a current or former CIA contractor and described it as comparable in scale and significance to the information Edward Snowden gave to reporters in 2013.

No one has challenged the authenticity of the original documents of Vault 7, which disclosed a vast array of cyber warfare tools developed, probably with help from NSA, by CIA's Engineering Development Group. That Group was part of the sprawling CIA Directorate of Digital Innovation—a growth industry established by John Brennan in 2015.

Scarcely imaginable digital tools—that can take control of your car and make it race over 100 mph, for example, or can enable remote spying through a TV—were described and duly reported in the *New York Times* and other media throughout March. But the Vault 7, part 3 release on March 31 that exposed the "Marble Framework" program apparently was judged too delicate to qualify as "news fit to print" and was kept out of the *Times*.

The Washington Post's Ellen Nakashima, it seems, "did not get the memo" in time. Her March 31 article bore the catching (and accurate) headline: **WikiLeaks' latest release of CIA cyber-tools could blow the cover on agency hacking operations.**

The WikiLeaks release indicated that Marble was designed for flexible and easy-to-use "obfuscation," and that Marble source code includes a "deobfuscator" to reverse CIA text obfuscation.

More important, the CIA reportedly used Marble during 2016. In her *Washington Post* report, Nakashima left that out, but did include another significant point made by WikiLeaks; namely, that the obfuscation tool could be used to conduct a "forensic attribution double game" or false-flag operation because it included test samples in Chinese, Russian, Korean, Arabic and Farsi.

The CIA's reaction was neuralgic. Director Mike Pompeo lashed out two weeks later, calling Assange and his associates "demons," and insisting, "It's time to call out WikiLeaks for what it really is, a non-state hostile intelligence service, often abetted by state actors like Russia."

Mr. President, we do not know if CIA's Marble Framework, or tools like it, played some kind of role in the campaign to blame Russia for hacking the DNC. Nor do we know how candid the denizens of CIA's Digital Innovation Directorate have been with you and with Director Pompeo. These are areas that might profit from early White House review.

Putin and the Technology

We also do not know if you have discussed cyber issues in any detail with President Putin. In his interview with NBC's Megyn Kelly, he seemed quite willing—perhaps even eager—to address issues related to

kremlin.ru

President Vladimir Putin answers questions from NBC anchor Megyn Kelly on the sidelines of the St. Petersburg International Economic Forum, June 5, 2017.

the kind of cyber tools revealed in the Vault 7 disclosures, if only to indicate he has been briefed on them. Putin pointed out that today's technology enables hacking to be "masked and camouflaged to an extent that no one can understand the origin" [of the hack]. And, vice versa, it is possible to set up any entity or any individual that everyone will think that they are the exact source of that attack."

"Hackers may be anywhere," he said. "There may be hackers, by the way, in the United States who very craftily and professionally passed the buck to Russia. Can't you imagine such a scenario? ... I can."

Full Disclosure: Over recent decades the ethos of our intelligence profession has eroded in the public mind to the point that agenda-free analysis is deemed well nigh impossible. Thus, we add this disclaimer, which applies to everything we in VIPS say and do: We have no political agenda; our sole purpose is to spread truth around and, when necessary, hold to account our former intelligence colleagues.

We speak and write without fear or favor. Consequently, any resemblance between what we say and what presidents, politicians and pundits say is purely coincidental. The fact we find it is necessary to include that reminder speaks volumes about these highly politicized times. This is our 50th VIPS Memorandum since the afternoon of Powell's speech at the UN. Live links to the 49 past memos can be found at https://consortiumnews.com/vips-memos/.

FOR THE STEERING GROUP,
VETERAN INTELLIGENCE
PROFESSIONALS FOR SANITY

William Binney, former NSA Technical Director for World Geopolitical & Military Analysis; Co-founder of NSA's Signals Intelligence Automation Research Center

Skip Folden, independent analyst, retired IBM Program Manager for Information Technology US (Associate VIPS)

Matthew Hoh, former Capt., USMC, Iraq & Foreign Service Officer, Afghanistan (associate VIPS)

Larry C Johnson, CIA & State Department (ret.)

Michael S. Kearns, Air Force Intelligence Officer (Ret.), Master SERE Resistance to Interrogation Instructor

John Kiriakou, Former CIA Counterterrorism Officer and former Senior Investigator, Senate Foreign Relations Committee

Linda Lewis, WMD preparedness policy analyst, USDA (ret.)

Lisa Ling, TSgt USAF (ret.) (associate VIPS)

Edward Loomis, Jr., former NSA Technical Director for the Office of Signals Processing

David MacMichael, National Intelligence Council (ret.)

Ray McGovern, former U.S. Army Infantry/Intelligence officer and CIA analyst

Elizabeth Murray, former Deputy National Intelligence Officer for Middle East, CIA

Coleen Rowley, FBI Special Agent and former Minneapolis Division Legal Counsel (ret.)

Cian Westmoreland, former USAF Radio Frequency Transmission Systems Technician and Unmanned Aircraft Systems whistleblower (Associate VIPS)

Kirk Wiebe, former Senior Analyst, SIGINT Automation Research Center, NSA

Sarah G. Wilton, Intelligence Officer, DIA (ret.); Commander, US Naval Reserve (ret.)

Ann Wright, U.S. Army Reserve Colonel (ret) and former U.S. Diplomat